# AGE OF
# ENLIGHTENMENT

TIME
LIFE
BOOKS

GREAT AGES OF MAN

*A History of the World's Cultures*

# AGE OF ENLIGHTENMENT

by

PETER GAY

and

The Editors of TIME-LIFE BOOKS

TIME-LIFE BOOKS, AMSTERDAM

THE AUTHOR: Peter Gay is a professor of history at Yale University and a well-known authority on European intellectual history and political philosophy. Born in Germany, he was educated in the United States and received his doctoral degree in government at Columbia in 1951. He has been associated with the university ever since, except for a year's research fellowship at Princeton. He is the author of *The Party of Humanity: Essays in the French Enlightenment; Voltaire's Politics: The Poet as Realist;* and *The Dilemma of Democratic Socialism.* Professor Gay's *The Enlightenment: An Interpretation* received a 1967 National Book Award.

THE CONSULTING EDITOR: Leonard Krieger, now University Professor of Modern History at the University of Chicago, was formerly Professor of History at Yale and Columbia universities. Dr. Krieger is the author of *The German Idea of Freedom* and *The Politics of Discretion,* and is co-author of *History,* written in collaboration with John Higham and Felix Gilbert.

THE COVER: This painting by Pietro Longhi shows a bourgeois family taking a lesson in geography—one of many signs of the age's expanding intellectual horizons.

© 1966 Time-Life books Inc. All rights reserved.
Eighth European English language printing 1983.

ISBN 900658 29 0

TIME-LIFE is a trademark of Time Incorporated U.S.A.

# CONTENTS

NOTE: THE PRESENT LOCATIONS OF ALL WORKS OF ART REPRODUCED IN THIS BOOK ARE LISTED ON PAGES 186-187.

# PREFACE

During most of the 19th century, critics, philosophers, historians and artists all damned the 18th century as the "Age of Prose and Reason": one-sided, shallow, rationalistic, unable to understand man and the universe, a static rather than a dynamic culture. The range of their condemnations was great, from Wordsworth's reference to Voltair's *Candide* as "that dull product of a scoffer's pen" to James Russell Lowell's objection to the whole 18th century as "that razor-ridden age".

Our own generation has learned to look on the 18th century with less jaundiced vision. We can indeed produce so well balanced a treatment of the Enlightenment as this one of Peter Gay's. For, though Professor Gay likes the *philosophes* he writes about, and shares their basic belief in the ability to use thought to make this earth a better place, he is fully aware of the complexities of the Age of Enlightenment, knows its doubts, its fears, its own full awareness of how far man is from complete rationality, and its occasional understandable impatience with ordinary human limitations. He finds place in this book for the full range of the culture of the age, its important German phases, so often pushed into the background in English and American works on the subject, as well as its more familiar British and French phases. He manages, without bogging down in a mass of detail, to give the reader telling bits of the mind and heart of these enlightened thinkers, who were also, as he shows, often enlightened doers.

Here then, in remarkably succinct form, is the age which, more than any other, brought to some kind of focus in the awareness of millions (not just of a middle class) those revolutionary ideas we are still living with, still struggling for or against. Call this what you will—the Industrial Revolution, the democratic revolution, the scientific revolution, the intellectual revolution, or simply "modernization", "revolution of rising expectations", even "Americanization"—it is now world-wide.

Professor Gay brings out clearly the extent to which the *philosophes* of the Enlightenment rejected the traditional Christian picture of a universe divided between a City of God and a City of Earth. Louis de Saint-Just, the youthful French revolutionary, put it neatly in a speech to the Convention: "Happiness is a new idea in Europe". And he was talking not simply about ultimate happiness in another and heavenly world, but about the concept of happiness in the here and now. But Professor Gay also shows the extent to which most people, including at bottom the *philosophes* themselves, continued to accept the basic tenets of the Western Judeo-Christian tradition.

The 19th century, although it was extremely critical of the Enlightenment, still kept much of its predecessor's faith in the possibility of progress towards a better world. Many of the intellectuals of our own century, faced with two world wars, a great depression, an apparently unending and not really very cold war, have sometimes seemed to reject more completely than the romantic generation of 1800 ever did the whole heritage of the Enlightenment. However, that heritage is clearly alive among millions, West and East, even in the midst of all the horrors of our present Time of Troubles. For, to revert to Arnold Toynbee's famous figure of the climbers on the cliff, our Western civilization really did in the Age of Enlightenment begin to edge itself precariously upwards on to a new foothold. It is still there.

CRANE BRINTON

*Harvard University*

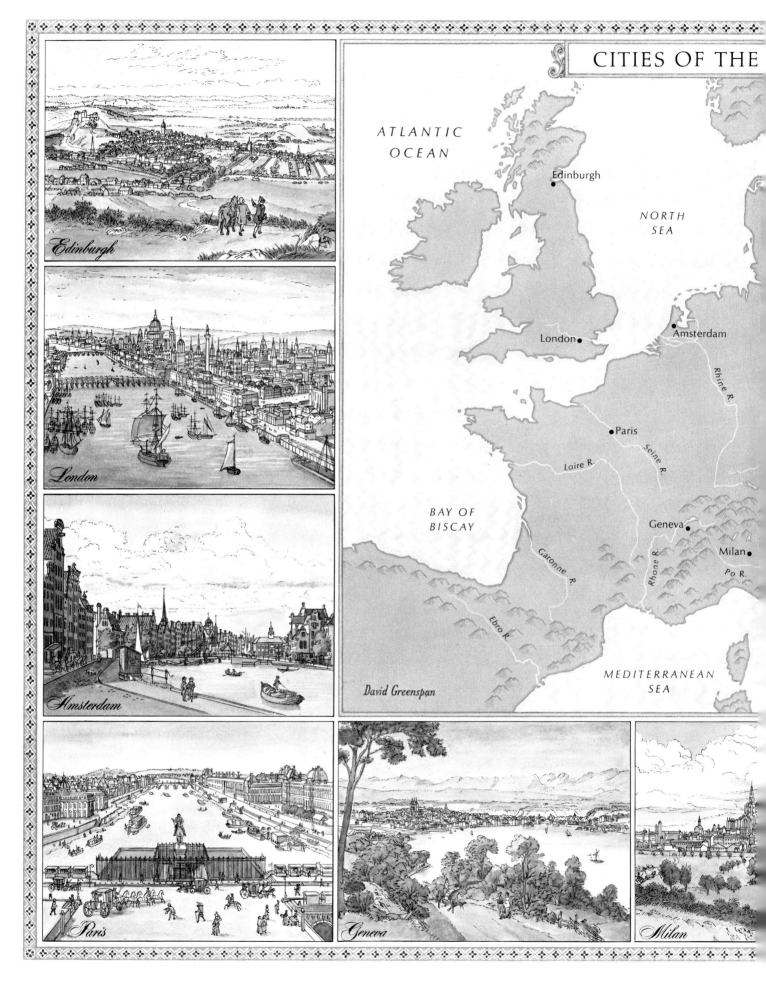

Edinburgh

London

Amsterdam

Paris

Geneva

Milan

# CITIES OF THE

ATLANTIC
OCEAN

NORTH
SEA

Edinburgh

London

Amsterdam

Rhine R.

Paris

Loire R.

Seine R.

BAY OF
BISCAY

Garonne R.

Geneva

Rhone R.

Milan

Po R.

Ebro R.

MEDITERRANEAN
SEA

David Greenspan

# ENLIGHTENMENT

BALTIC SEA

St. Petersburg

Berlin

Weimar

Vistula R.

Dnieper R.

Elbe R.

Danube R.

Vienna

Dniester R.

Danube R.

BLACK SEA

Florence

ADRIATIC SEA

SCALE

0   50   100   150 Miles

St. Petersburg

Berlin

Weimar

Florence

Vienna

# 1
# THE PRACTICAL PHILOSOPHERS

In 1784, at the height of the Age of Enlightenment, the German philosopher Immanuel Kant wrote an article for a popular audience explaining the meaning of the word that gave the age its name. "Enlightenment", Kant began, "is man's emergence from his nonage." This nonage, or immaturity, he continued, was caused not by "lack of intelligence, but lack of determination and courage to use that intelligence without another's guidance. *Sapere aude!* Dare to know! Have the courage to use your own intelligence!".

Kant's words summed up the most cherished convictions and ambitious designs of radical 18th-century scholars and intellectuals. His words implied that man was mature enough to find his own way without paternal authority; they urged man to understand his own nature and the natural world by the methods of science. In short, they were a declaration of freedom. Kant and his fellow thinkers wanted men to shake off the hand of authority in politics and religion, and think for themselves.

Kant was called a *philosophe*, a French word that did not apply to Frenchmen alone. From Scotland to Naples an impressive clan of radical intellectuals had become passionate and outspoken partisans of the new philosophy of John Locke and the new science of Isaac Newton. They were hostile to organized Christianity, and said so; they openly deplored cruel legal procedures and arbitrary government; they believed in freedom of speech and the press, and in personal liberty. They were erudite, but they were not above popularizing their views. Kant's article had been preceded by a vigorous campaign conducted by the *philosophes* in country after country, designed to expose the evils of religion and extol the virtues of their own enlightened philosophy.

And yet, while the *philosophes* were a clan, they were not a coherent movement. Although they knew one another and corresponded, they did not always think alike. The only thing they had in common was a critical attitude towards any sort of orthodoxy, and especially towards orthodox religion. They did not believe in miracles, and, if they believed in God at all, thought of Him as the mechanic of the universe—a sort of cosmic watchmaker; He had built a superb machine, given it laws to run by and then withdrawn. From such a view it followed that the only reliable road to knowledge of God's plans was through science, not religion, through observation and experiment, not dogma and revelation.

Fortunately for the *philosophes'* purpose, their ideas were launched in a cultural atmosphere that was generally favourable to them. Thousands of educated men and women who were good Christians and thoroughly loyal to existing, political institutions—men and women, in fact, who had nothing but dislike, and even contempt, for the *philosophes* —nevertheless shared at least some of their attitudes. They were humanitarians, or tepid about religious observances, or critical of government policies. The *philosophes* had many allies who did not know they were allies, people whose cast of mind was compatible with the ultimate goals of the Enlightenment.

Clearly, an age that takes its name from an intellectual atmosphere cannot be fixed within rigid chronological limits. In one sense the Enlightenment began as far back as the Renaissance, with men's renewed interest in Greek and Latin texts, their critical approach to medieval Christian philosophy and their general sense of curiosity about this world as opposed to the next. Even the Protestant Reformation, despite its call for a return to the beliefs of early Christianity, helped to prepare the way for the Enlightenment by disrupting the unit of Western Christendom and weakening the authority of the Church.

During the 17th century, philosophers tried to weld the consequences of these intellectual developments into a new kind of philosophy, distinct from the Christian world-view of medieval theologians. It was this century, too, that elaborated the new science—and without science and reason the Enlightenment would have been unthinkable. In fact, if a single point in time must be assigned as the

start of the Enlightenment, no date could be more logical and fitting than the year of Newton's publication of his widely admired—but intellectually demanding—masterpiece, the *Philosophiae naturalis principia mathematica (Mathematical Principles of Natural Philosophy)*. That year was 1687.

In 1687, what was Europe like? France, the most powerful country in Europe, was in the middle of the long reign of Louis XIV, the Sun King, a man of considerable ability and vast aspirations. Louis built himself impressive palaces, reigned over a glittering court at Versailles, and encouraged the arts and literature with notable success. All across the Continent, rulers powerful and petty imitated him by posing as gentlemen of refinement and benefactors of culture.

But Louis was a menace, as well as a model. He strengthened the powers of the central government and silenced domestic criticism. He revoked the century-old Edict of Nantes, which had granted tolerance to French Huguenots, driving them out of France by the thousands to settle in England, Prussia, the Netherlands and America. He built himself an imposing army and in a ruthless series of military actions expanded French power to the north and east.

In 1687, the year that Newton published his *Principia*, Louis was acquisitively eyeing the Rhineland and was even casting glances towards oncepowerful Spain, now rapidly declining under its sickly monarch Charles II (of whom it was said, rather cruelly, that he was perpetually dying). Thus France was technically at peace but the rest of Europe, knowing it to be but a lull, was preparing for war. The League of Augsburg, a coalition of European powers, was preparing itself to face a French monarch who, for all his passion for culture and all his devotion to reason in administrative affairs, was much closer to being a despot than an enlightened ruler.

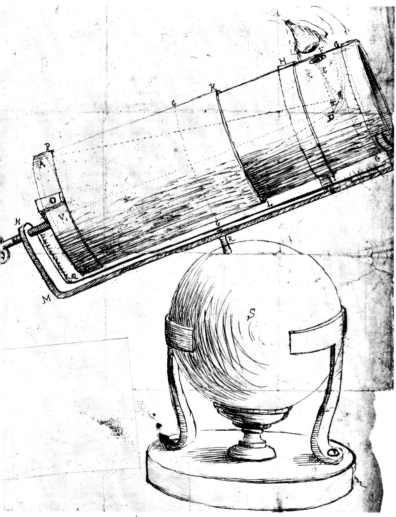

NEWTON'S REFLECTING TELESCOPE, *built from his own sketch (above), was only six inches long, but it could magnify objects as powerfully with mirrors as an ordinary six-foot telescope of the day could with its primitive, light-scattering lenses. Like many modern telescopes, its curved mirror (A, upper left) focused images on to a smaller flat mirror (D, upper right) which aimed them into the eyepiece (F, top). The screw (N, left) was used to adjust the telescope's focal length. A large ball joint (S) supported the device.*

In 1687 England, soon to be France's greatest enemy, was its abject dependent. Its Roman Catholic King, James II, hampered by a close-fisted parliament, was forced to depend on France for subsidies and support. James was unable to confine himself to the private practice of a faith that most of his countrymen feared and despised. He tried to bring England back into the Roman fold by purging anti-Catholic masters from the colleges and introducing Catholics into the government and the army. In 1688 James had an heir, and Englishmen, unable to stand the thought of being governed by a Catholic house, expelled both James and his heir and installed Protestant monarchs, William III and Mary. In the new atmosphere English science and philosophy flourished, making England the first home of the Enlightenment and a model for intellectuals on the Continent.

Meanwhile, a large segment of that continent, the Holy Roman Empire, lay sunk in torpor. It was more a memory or a joke than a political reality, a crazy quilt of more than 300 separate States—most of them minute—governed more or less autonomously by vest-pocket dukes, autocratic ecclesiastics or narrow-minded burghers. Few of these States could have afforded a theatre, even if they had wanted one. Few could, or would, support the work of writers or scholars. In 1687 while other States were beginning to move towards the age of the Great Powers, the Holy Roman Empire remained a haphazard collection of small powers connected more by a name than any orderly political structure.

The Empire did include, however, some of the lands of two large family domains: the empire of the Habsburgs, ruled by Leopold I, and the Brandenburg-Prussian empire of the Hohenzollerns, ruled by Frederick William, the Great Elector. Leopold controlled not only Austria and Bohemia, but had recently reconquered Hungary from the Turks. Both he and his successors were too busy with gov-

GOSSIP AND FELLOWSHIP *flourished in London's 17th and 18th-century coffee-houses, augmenting the Enlightenment's communications explosion. Here writers, businessmen, scientists and politicians would come to find out what was going on.*

ernment affairs, however, to interest themselves in the new ideas circulating to the west. And although Brandenburg-Prussia, nearing the end of Frederick William's long reign, was clearly on the way to challenging its neighbours, Berlin was still an insignificant town. Not until a later Hohenzollern, Frederick William's great-grandson Frederick the Great, ascended the throne in 1740 was Prussia to be hospitable to the Enlightenment.

A perceptive observer, looking about him in 1687, would probably have predicted that if there was to be an enlightenment, it would begin in the then-fertile intellectual climate of England, would move from there to the ready soil of France, and would then spread throughout Europe and even to the European colonies in America. That is what a perceptive observer would have said, and he would have been right.

Isaac Newton of England did not, however, step upon an empty stage. The Scientific Revolution, like most revolutions in man's way of looking at the world, was rooted deep in the past; Newton had many ancestors. The critical impulse upon which science depends was first liberated by the ancient Greek philosophers who passed it on to their disciples, the Romans. Not even the Middle Ages' preference for theology over philosophy wholly stifled it. For the sake of better harvests, for the sake of trade and navigation, medieval men studied the properties of natural materials and the geography of the earth.

Besides, there were good religious reasons for studying science. Just as the Bible and Church dogma gave men a knowledge of God's word, so the study of the natural world gave them a knowledge of His works. As early as the 13th century, Roger Bacon, a Franciscan friar, evolved an elaborate plan for the conduct of research which was essentially the scientific method: investigate, experiment. Bacon justified his plan by asserting that since the creation of the world was God's handiwork, studying that world could be considered a form of piety.

But the accumulated discoveries and theories that are justly called the Scientific Revolution had to await later, more favourable conditions. They came, these new and better times, in the closing days of the Renaissance, and chiefly in Italy. Humanist scholars, avid to restore the classical texts of ancient Greece and Rome, revived not only their literary masterpieces but also their treatises on the natural world. The rediscovered works of such men as the second-century Roman physician Galen awakened a keen new interest in nature. And in looking at nature more frankly and directly than their medieval predecessors had done, the Renaissance humanists opened the way to a more precise observation of the world. The masterly anatomical drawings of Leonardo da Vinci, compared with the mis-shapen sketches of men and animals by the French architect Villard de Honnecourt, 300 years before, reflect the dawn of a world more hospitable to science.

Finally, and perhaps most significantly, the humanists, with their critical intellects, began to topple the authoritarian structure of medieval thought that had governed, and crippled, scientific investigation. For centuries things had been held to be true in science because Aristotle had said they were true. Sometimes the humanists were very little more adventurous; at first they simply substituted Galen's authority for Aristotle's. But at least, in pitting one authority against another, they opened a door to freedom. More and more, as the 16th century progressed, men began to think, if not to say, that things were true in science because their own experience told them so—through observation and experiment.

This initial cautiousness about investigating nature did not stem from fear, but from philosophers' training in traditional lore and traditional methods.

For all their boldness, the two most revolutionary works in 16th-century science looked both forward and backward. Nicholas Copernicus's *Concerning the Revolutions of the Heavenly Bodies* and Andreas Vesalius's *Concerning the Fabric of the Human Body* were, curiously enough, published in the same year, 1543. Copernicus substituted a stationary sun for a stationary earth in his system of the universe, and thus became the father of modern astronomy. But his rotating planets still retained their time-honoured circular orbits because the circle was the perfect geometrical figure—and it was difficult to think of natural law as other than perfect. Similarly, Vesalius's superb descriptions of the human body, drawn directly from his own medical experience, surpassed those of all previous anatomists in accuracy of detail and daring of method. Yet Vesalius worshipped Galen, and at first thought that when his observations did not coincide with Galen's it was because he had made a mistake: his observations, not Galen's, were in error.

It was only in the 17th century that science finally broke loose from the moorings of tradition. For all the mystical beauty of the circle, and in spite of his predilection for mysticism, the German astronomer Johannes Kepler calculated the orbits of the planets to be ellipses. Kepler's brave step forward was matched by others—Galileo's remarkable theories about the behaviour of moving bodies, William Harvey's discovery of the circulation of the blood—and by the construction of various philosophical systems to explain and justify the new scientific procedures.

This coalition of science and philosophy was of decisive importance to the Scientific Revolution: it led the best minds of the age into scientific inquiry and gave science the sanction of reason. It made the work of Galileo, Robert Boyle and Newton not a series of accidental discoveries, but steps in a cumulative process. And it provided the underlying principle for the whole Enlightenment.

The greatest of these 17th-century scientific philosophers were René Descartes, Galileo Galilei and Francis Bacon. Descartes was French, a brilliant mathematician and an imaginative theorizer about the nature of man and the universe. He made notable contributions to the sciences of optics, physics, physiology and psychology, and he is considered the father of modern analytical geometry. But none of these contributions is as important as the contribution of his intellectual method, which today is known as Cartesian thought.

Descartes' search for a new method grew out of a desire to resolve the endless disputes of philosophers over every conceivable issue. He wanted to build a view of the world that all rational men would accept. In the course of his search he developed certain revolutionary rules of reasoning which he claimed could be used for solving any complex problem. The student of nature, he argued, must discard all questionable preconceptions and begin his intellectual constructions from "clear and distinct" ideas. Then he can move, step by cautious step, from these ideas to others, and thus build up a logical universe. Descartes himself began this construction with the famous *cogito, ergo sum*—"I think, therefore I am".

But this was not all. Descartes did not disdain empirical research; in fact he enjoyed making observations and experiments. But his emphasis was on the abstract character of science. He argued that mathematics was the one language capable of expressing scientific ideas with complete clarity. Partly through his assiduous propaganda for it, and partly through his own successes with it, he convinced other philosophers. It became customary to think of scientific inquiries as mathematical in nature, and of scientific laws as mathematical in form.

Galileo, his Italian contemporary, emphasized observation: he preferred looking to abstract speculation. In Galileo's day most professors of natural science still believed and taught Aristotle's theories about matter and motion, theories that were then 2,000 years old. Galileo urged the professors to look through his perfected telescope and see for themselves: the universe was not to be understood from theories, but from observing the thing itself. Scientific speculation, pleaded Galileo, should be directed by facts. But he wisely added that men should not trust sense impressions alone; the laws of the universe must also be sought through mathematical models—formulae and equations.

Besides being a persuasive propagandist, Galileo was also an impressive practising scientist. He discovered four of the satellites of Jupiter, the irregularity of the surface of the moon, and the fact that the Milky Way was made up of numberless stars. He discovered the phases of Venus and, in company with other astronomers, the spots on the sun. His experiments and theories in the field of mechanics were even more important, culminating in his theory of inertia. Mathematician, experimenter, instrument-maker, polemic and dreamer, Galileo left a legacy of ideas that changed men's notions about the universe once and for all.

Compared to him, Francis Bacon seems curiously one-sided. Bacon was a moralist and prophet; his scientific writings are studded with aphorisms and he was mainly concerned with guiding men in the right scientific procedures. But it is wrong to view him, as critics sometimes do, simply as a fact-finder, or to imagine that the goal of his scientific energies was simply human comfort. Bacon said that for centuries philosophers had acted like ants, diligently but stupidly gathering little, useless bits of knowledge—or like spiders, spinning out intricate, unsubstantial theories from their own insides. The true philosopher, he said, must be like a bee; he must go to nature for his raw materials and absorb nature's lessons, and then, through exacting

A BALLOONIST'S ODYSSEY, *Jean-Pierre Blanchard's 250-mile jaunt from Lille to Servon in 1785 was one of several early voyages that opened men's eyes to the possibilities of flight. This chart of Blanchard's journey notes altitudes and events en route. On the left, a dog leaves the gondola ("chute du chien"); this is followed by* *lunch below the clouds, some letters airmailed over the side, an unexplained dip close to the ground, then an exquisite leap above the clouds—during which Blanchard's companion, de L'Epinard, took a nap (until thunder and lightning presumably woke him). Europeans were soon talking of balloons as weapons to end wars.*

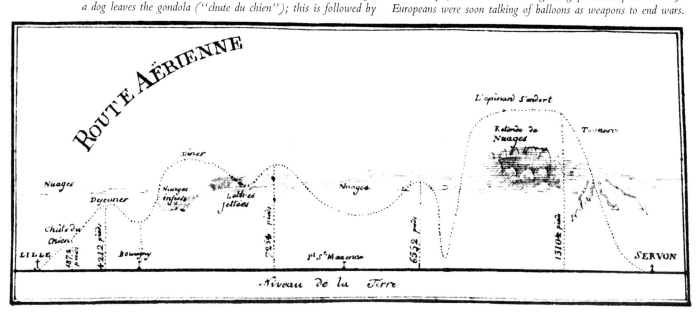

labour, transform these lessons into sound theories.

Although Bacon considered knowledge in itself to be a virtue, his great hope was that men would use the new knowledge to achieve power over nature, and thus lead happier, healthier, longer lives. "The true and lawful goal of the sciences", he wrote, "is none other than this: that human life be endowed with new discoveries and power." It was a glorious dream and an enormously influential one. All through the 17th and 18th centuries radical intellectuals all over Europe proudly allied themselves with him: Denis Diderot's famous *Encyclopédie*, published in instalments between 1751 and 1772, practically made Bacon its patron saint.

Of Bacon's many fertile suggestions for the improvement of science, probably the most fruitful one was his proposal that scientific research be made a collaborative venture. In *The New Atlantis*, his blueprint for a Utopian society, he includes an academy of scientists, liberally provided with brains and funds. A few such academies already existed when Bacon wrote, but after *Atlantis* they sprang

up everywhere. All of them were endowed with vigour and good will, but not all of them were adequately financed. The most important of them was the English society which, after passing through several preliminary phases, was finally chartered in 1662 as the Royal Society of London for the Improvement of Natural Knowledge.

The Royal Society lived up to its name. It held meetings to encourage scientific inquiry, engaged in correspondence in aid of the "new philosophy", and reported on experiments, discoveries and inventions in its famous publication, *Philosophical Transactions*.

Every prominent natural philosopher in England belonged to it, and so did many distinguished scientists on the Continent. So, too, did gifted amateurs like the diarist Samuel Pepys and the American statesman-scientist Benjamin Franklin. The list of its Fellows is a list of the leaders of the Scientific Revolution, but the greatest name on the list was that of Isaac Newton.

When Newton stepped upon the scene, the stage

was set and his role prepared. His work is the culmination of a century's efforts—of Bacon's method, Galileo's mechanics, Descartes' mathematics, and the scientific endeavours of his Fellows in the Royal Society. But for all he owed to others, Newton's own achievement was tremendous and his contemporaries knew it: they first admired him, then idolized him. Alexander Pope's celebrated couplet sums up his impact on his age:

*Nature and Nature's Laws lay hid in Night:*
*God said, "Let Newton be!" and all was Light.*

Newton was born in 1642, the year Galileo died. Even as a youth he was a precocious mathematician, but no one thought of him as a genius. At Cambridge University he was considered to be intelligent, but rather absent-minded. Then in 1665, when he was 22, he went home to Lincolnshire to escape the Great Plague raging through London and threatening Cambridge. There in isolation, he mused about the universe and made his greatest discoveries. "I was in the prime of my age for invention," he later recalled, "and minded mathematics and philosophy more than at any time since."

In a year and a half, between 1665 and 1667, Newton worked out the essentials of the branch of mathematics called calculus, hit upon the crucially important optical law that white light is a mixture of colours, and, most significant of all, grasped the principle of the law of gravitation—by observing, so the story goes, a falling apple in a garden.

But Newton was more interested in research than in fame, and for years he published none of these findings. The invitation to join the Royal Society was based on his improvements in the telescope. It was not until 1687, at the urging of his friend, the astronomer Edmund Halley, that he published his *Principia mathematica*. The *Principia*, which in Newton's own words accounts for all "the motions of the planets, the comets, the moon, and the sea", is probably the greatest scientific work ever written. It completed the revolution begun by Copernicus in the 16th century, and dominated scientific thought for more than 200 years.

After its publication Newton paid the frequent price of fame: he became embroiled in bitter quarrels over precedence of discoveries. Then, in the 1690's, he suffered an alarming mental breakdown characterized by delusions of persecution. Yet he recovered enough to become president of the Royal Society, and to publish, in 1704, his *Opticks*, a work filled with pioneering insights into the physical characteristics of light. *Opticks* concludes with a series of provocative questions, "in order", as Newton put it, to "farther search to be made by others". Among them is the perceptive suggestion that light can behave like particles of matter. When he died in 1727, Newton was buried at Westminster Abbey in a funeral whose pallbearers included two dukes, three earls and the Lord Chancellor—like a king, as Voltaire put it, who had been good to his subjects.

Almost a century later, inspired by Newton's statue in Cambridge, the poet William Wordsworth wrote of "his prism and silent face" and of his voyaging "through strange seas of thought, alone". This is not strictly true: like other great innovators, Newton had both ancestors and companions—scientists whom he read and scientists with whom he talked. And yet, in a sense, Wordsworth was right. Newton alone grasped what dozens of brilliant searchers before him had glimpsed only in part: that heaven and earth were a single system governed by the same laws. If the word "genius" had been coined to describe a single man, that man might well have been Newton.

Newton also acted like a genius in another way: like many brilliant men, he was eccentric. He hated publicity and loathed controversy—so much so that

AN HEROIC NEWTON, *encumbered only by a drawing compass and a scroll, strikes a romantic ''scientist's'' pose in this sketch by the mystical, anti-scientific poet and painter William Blake. Sitting on a rock in a sea of time and space, he intently defines with his mathematical instruments the facts of the material world. Blake recognized Newton's genius but cried: "God is not a mathematical diagram!".*

he frequently got his friends to publish his papers and conduct his arguments for him. He was also odd in his religious views and intensely interested in alchemy. He spent untold hours reading Egyptian and Hebrew history, trying to fix the dates of Biblical events right back to the Creation. And some of the notes in his private papers suggest that he seriously believed in the elixir of life and the existence of a philosophers' stone.

These oddities in Newton's character caused some gossip, but everyone agreed, nevertheless, that his discoveries made him one of the great scientists of history. And yet, curiously, Newton's lasting renown rests less on his discoveries than on his method. Newton himself, in fact, took pains to publicize his method whenever he could. In a letter addressed to the secretary of the Royal Society of 1672, he wrote that "The best and safest method of philosophizing seems to be, first, to inquire diligently into the properties of things and to establish those properties by experiments, and to proceed later to hypotheses for the explanation of things themselves. For hypotheses ought to be applied only in the explanation of the properties of things, and not made use of in determining them".

Newton's own slogan, *hypotheses non fingo*—"I do not invent hypotheses"—became the slogan of several generations of philosophers and scientists. But to Newton, and to his 18th-century followers, the word "hypothesis" had a special meaning. It was not just a tentative statement suggesting a course of inquiry, but a wholly imaginary thought construction—in Newton's words, "a proposition as is not a phenomenon nor deduced from any phenomenon, but assumed or supposed—without any experimental proof". It was, in short, a kind of metaphysical make-believe, and Newton was cautioning men not to use such imaginary systems of thought as the foundation upon which to base further inquiries.

Unfortunately, Newton's own theory of gravitation, with its suggestion that bodies were drawn to each other by some sort of mutual attraction, smacked of the very metaphysics he deplored. His critics accused him of smuggling "occult qualities" into science—a harsh accusation, for "occult qualities" was a term of derision normally used by the new scientists to put down the "essences" and "quiddities" that sprinkled the writings of medieval scholars. Newton defended himself by pointing out that the effects of gravitation could be seen, and therefore could not be called occult. Furthermore, he said that while he did not pretend to understand the nature of gravitation, he could—on the basis of his observations and experiments—justifiably generalize about its behaviour.

Today this attitude is a commonplace among scientists, but in Newton's day it was a novelty, and it made an enormous and lasting impression on philosophers in two ways. It led them to prize the "scientific method"—the method of observation, generalization, experimentation—above all other methods of inquiry. And it led them to proclaim what they called, a little misleadingly, their "philosophical modesty": the world, they said, was full of mysteries and unanswered questions, and sensible men did not try to explain their causes, but, instead, paid attention to their effects. Newton, wrote Voltaire, taught men to "examine, weigh, calculate and measure, but never to conjecture. . . . He saw, and made people see; but he didn't put his fancies in place of truth".

These two consequences of Newton's work—confidence in the scientific method and modesty about man's capacity to know—appear at first to be contradictory. But they do come together, and it is precisely where they join that the energy for the Enlightenment arose. Newtonian thought meant, first of all, that only patient and sceptical inquiry could produce reliable results. The vaulting philosophical systems of 17th-century metaphysicians, and the improbable tales of saints and miracle-workers, were equally suspect and equally useless.

Secondly, Newtonian thought meant that the scientific method could, with care, be applied to non-scientific disciplines—to theology, history, morals,

politics. Thirdly, Newtonian thought meant that men did not have to concern themselves with airy fantasies about first causes, but could instead concentrate their intellectual energies on practical problems, on improving man's lot in this world. This is how the *philosophes* understood Bacon: thinking, they said, must bear useful fruit; talk must be to some practical purpose.

Newton would have been deeply shocked by some of the conclusions the *philosophes* reached using his scientific method. He would have despised the deists, who turned God into a master mechanic, and would have been outraged by the atheists, who denied Him altogether. But then, not all the *philosophes* were wholly comfortable with Newton either. They found the language of mathematics too obscure and disliked the rigour of Newtonian thought. For every devout Newtonian, like Voltaire or Kant or Locke, there were many who gave him no more than pious lip service.

Between the two extremes there were others, like Diderot, who were devoted to Newton more from a general sympathy with the direction of his thought than from a detailed mastery of its parts. Admiring the immense prestige that science had acquired, they took the scientific attitude for their own. With science as a licence they proceeded to examine all men's assertions in all fields of knowledge with critical freedom. They also took it as a philosophical position wholly incompatible with divine revelation. On this point all the men of the Enlightenment agreed, however much they knew of Newton and wherever they lived. David Hume in Scotland, Immanuel Kant in Prussia, Denis Diderot in Paris, Cesare Beccaria in Milan—all of them believed that when science advanced, religion had to retreat. Thus the uneasy peace between reason and revelation became war, and the Scientific Revolution was turned into an open rebellion against the faith that had governed Europe for more than a thousand years.

PLAYING AT SCIENCE, *English gentry peer into the wrong ends of telescopes, while a fop with a magnifying glass stares foolishly at a celestial sphere.*

# THE GENTLEMAN
# SCIENTISTS

In the 18th century men examined the world around them with less dogma or preconception than any men since the ancient Greeks. It was, philosopher Alfred North Whitehead later wrote, "as though the very heavens were being opened". Naturalists collected and classified thousands of animals and plants. Geologists began to map the earth's crust. Chemists explained the phenomenon of burning, the nature of air and the composition of water, and showed chemistry the way to modern quantitative analysis. But the most fascinating aspect of what has been called the Enlightenment's "reckless search for truth" was that it was pursued largely by amateurs. England's George III took up botany; Portugal's John V studied astronomy. Lesser figures followed the fashion, collecting fossils, insects and dried plants. Even the ladies were swept up in the new craze. Voltaire's mistress wrote on gravitation, Paris socialite Mlle. de Coigny studied anatomy; Madame de Pompadour pondered the stars. Much of this activity was superficial, but some of it was profound—and out of it the foundations of modern science were built.

# BRINGING ORDER TO THE NATURAL WORLD

THE BUTTON-BUSH FLOWER *was called "Cephalanthus occidentalis" by Carl Linnaeus in his "Systema naturae". The plant's name tells botanists that its blossoms are "head"-shaped and that it comes from the Western Hemisphere.*

In the natural sciences, exploration led to discovery and discovery led to an embarrassment of riches—thousands upon thousands of individual species of plants and animals. The urgent problem was to classify them. The first man to do this was the Swedish doctor Carl Linnaeus, who identified 12,100 species of living things. Dividing plants according to their sexual characteristics, he was able to fit them into 24 categories. To provide names more meaningful and precise, he also invented binary nomenclature: instead of using everyday names like "daisy", or "oak", he labelled all living things in a systematic way, first by genus (the family name) and then by species (the individual name). Linnaeus's classic *Systema naturae* went through 12 editions in his lifetime. His students roamed the world on Dutch East Indies ships and with explorers like Captain Cook, discovering new species such as the tree ferns, eucalyptus and breadfruit of the South Pacific.

If Linnaeus was the innovator, Georges Louis Leclerc de Buffon, a dandified petty nobleman, was the great popularizer. Possessed of an incisive style that he polished by writing for eight hours each day, Buffon produced the most widely read scientific work of the century, a 44-volume *Natural History*. In it Frenchmen found zoology and biology translated into precise yet fascinating prose. "He loves order and makes it everywhere", exclaimed an admirer. It was an epigraph for the age.

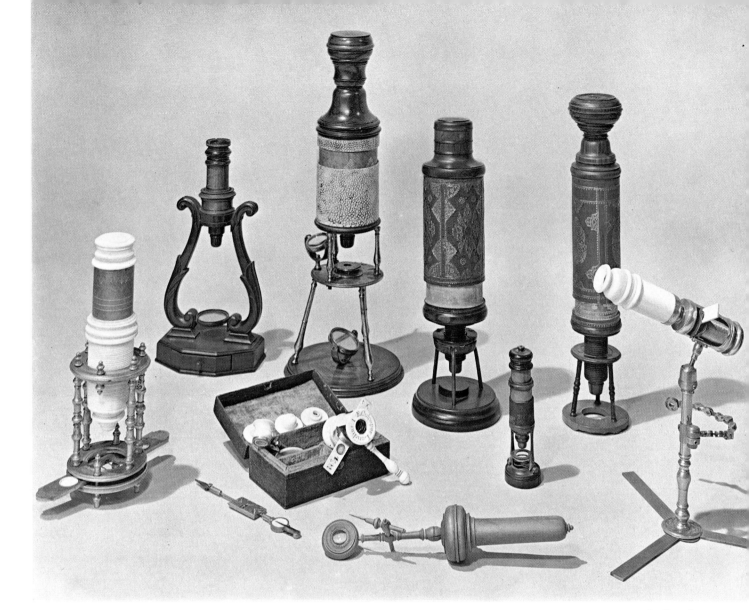

MAGNIFICENT MICROSCOPES, *ranging from elegant laboratory models (top) to portable naturalists' tools, were found in many private libraries and salons. When a rake in a play begged his "learned lady" to elope, she cried: "What! And leave my microscope?"*

JARDIN DES PLANTES, *which Buffon directed from 1739 to 1788, was internationally famous for its collection of exotic plants. To this Paris garden, which had 2,500 species as early as 1641, Buffon added natural-history galleries and a new chemistry laboratory.*

THE ANDROMEDA NEBULA *is one of the most important of the 2,500 nebulae and star clusters noted by the 18th-century astronomer William Herschel. His meticulous cataloguing helped to bring some notion of order to the baffling chaos beyond our own solar system.*

A MODEL SOLAR SYSTEM, *called an orrery, duplicated with clockwork the orbits of the earth and the moon around the sun (top, centre). Named after the Scottish Earl of Orrery by the instrument-maker John Rowley, these ornate toys graced many aristocratic drawing rooms.*

A PRIMITIVE PLANETARIUM *showing the zodiac and the planets intrigues children and adults during a talk on astronomy. As the painting suggests, the artist, Joseph Wright, was fascinated with the effects of light, not only as a painter but as an amateur scientist as well.*

# A NEW PERSPECTIVE ON THE STARS

The rational order so loved by the Enlightenment was nowhere more impressive than in the orderly heavens. In the 16th century Copernicus showed that the universe was not man-centred, that the earth revolved around the sun. In the 17th century, Galileo's telescope opened the universe to man's view; and Newton showed that this wondrously complex fabric of stars, planets and vast empty spaces moved with a clock-like predictability that human reason could reduce to a few simple equations. In the 18th century, William Herschel, an ex-oboist in the Hanoverian Guards, showed man how tiny he was in the cosmos by revealing to him a universe of a scale and grandeur never before imagined. Laboriously constructing the finest telescopes of his day, the self-made astronomer in 1781 found Uranus, the most distant planet discovered up to that time. Under Herschel's magnified scrutiny the so-called fixed stars were shown to be in motion, churning through space in sprawling galaxies. And he demonstrated that the Milky Way was not, as had been thought, a faint cloud of cosmic gas but an immense "lens-shaped" aggregation of separate stars—a galaxy, in fact, to which our sun belongs.

FIRE *was once thought to occur when matter gave off an inflammable "fluid" called phlogiston. Lavoisier showed instead that fire results when the element oxygen unites rapidly with matter.*

AIR *too thin for life suffocates a lark placed in a glass bell over an air pump, while spectators are instructed—and horrified. Such experiments helped to prove that oxygen was vital in respiration.*

# AN EXPLOSION IN CHEMISTRY

Even late in the age, scientists still thought air, water and fire to be indivisible elements and identified chemicals by kitchen names such as liver of sulphur, butter of arsenic and Glauber's salts. Then, touched by the Enlightenment's scientific explosion, the chemists began systematically to weigh, measure and test. Henry Cavendish isolated hydrogen; Joseph Black discovered carbon dioxide. The master, Antoine Lavoisier, established the doctrine of oxidation, solving the ancient mystery of fire. By proving that matter cannot be created or destroyed in chemical changes, Lavoisier further laid the groundwork for modern chemistry. No other scientists of the era matched the devotion of the chemists. In an age that believed firmly in trial and error, they were the greatest empiricists of all.

ANTOINE LAVOISIER, *the revolutionary who transformed chemistry, was himself, ironically, a victim of the French Revolution. Though he had urged reforms such as a free press, and taxes on the nobility, the mob remembered him as a one-time tax collector and land owner. He was guillotined in 1794.*

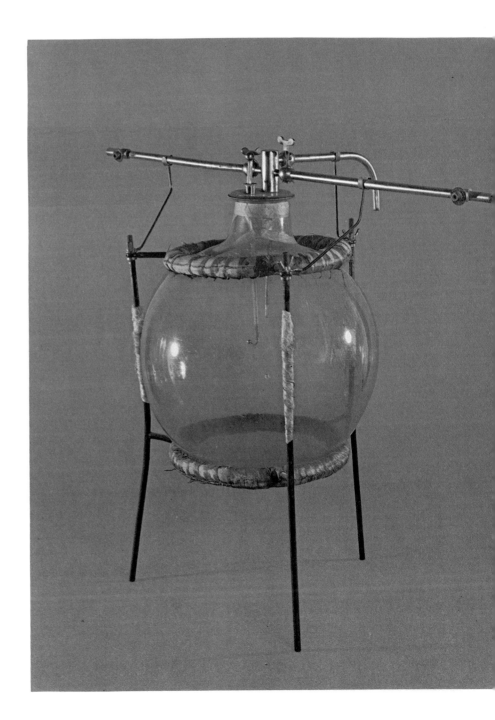

WATER, *Lavoisier knew, is compounded of oxygen and hydrogen. To demonstrate this he built the device on the right. The two gases entered the flask through the brass tubes and united chemically when exploded with an electric spark: there was a bang, and drops of water collected on the sides.*

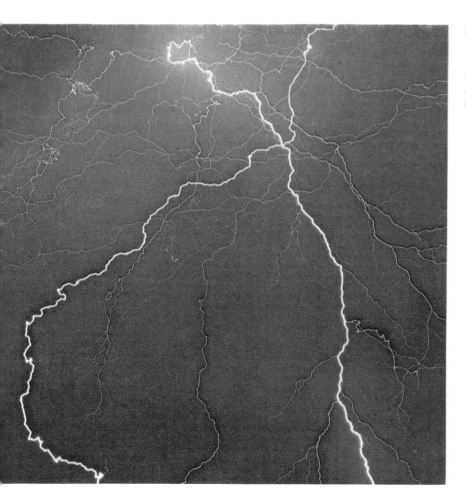

# ELECTRICITY BROUGHT TO EARTH

Experiments in electricity were the most amateurish, the most frivolous and the most fashionable of any attempted during the Enlightenment, yet the greatest strides in 18th-century physics were made in this field. With static electricity generators, Leyden jars (capacitors) and electrical circuits already known and easy to assemble, amateur "laboratories" sprang up everywhere. Many advances were accomplished by dilettantes, with their gadgets and party jokes. One of these, the "electric kiss", was the favourite of a German professor. He charged a pretty girl with static electricity; when men came forward to kiss her they got a shock that, as the scholar happily put it, nearly "broke their teeth".

More systematic experiments got under way at mid-century when Ben Franklin began to ask the crucial question: Just what is electricity? Though Franklin was a jokester too (he almost killed himself electrocuting a Christmas turkey), he had a sound grasp of scientific methods. He began to state hypotheses that could be tested by simple experiments. It was Franklin's "one-fluid" theory of electricity that eventually proved the truest explanation of the phenomenon that the age called "the electric virtue". Elected to the Royal Society, Franklin was worshipped in Europe as the embodiment of the new American—the son of liberty and of science. From a French contemporary came the dual tribute: "He snatched the lightning from the sky and the sceptre from the tyrant".

2

# A RELIGION
# OF RATIONALITY

CHURCHLY FRILLS *of the 18th century included glorious swarms of gilded cherubim and girlish angels, such as this one embellishing an abbey in Zwiefalten, Württemberg. Some thought that this "popular piety" was impious.*

For all the ferocity of the *philosophes'* attacks upon religion ("Let's eat some Jesuit", wrote Voltaire in *Candide*), the 18th century remained at bottom a religious age. The secular spirit of the Enlightenment by no means put an end to religion. What happened, rather, was that religious concerns were displaced—at least among the rich and well educated—from the centre of life to its periphery. This was partly the result of the *philosophes'* campaign against organized religion, and partly the result of the inroads made by Newtonian habits of thought.

But there were other agencies at work, too. Men were travelling more widely over the globe and discovering that there were other civilizations as advanced as their own. The claim of Christianity to be the one true faith was thrown into doubt; it seemed there might be some truth in other religions too. Men were also able, in the relative calm of the 18th century, to put aside the fear and uncertainty that goes with war and devote themselves to worldly pleasure.

But of all the things that pushed religious concerns to the periphery of 18th-century life, none perhaps may have been more powerful than the increasing secularization of religion itself. Caught up in the new spirit of rational inquiry, priests and ministers—Calvinists, Lutherans and Roman Catholics alike—began to examine the history of their own churches and those of their rivals with critical detachment and, often, sardonic scepticism. One monastic order would discount the claims of another to saintly deeds, and vice versa. Good Christians, watching these internecine disputes, were filled with mounting confusion. Their faith undermined, they offered the forces of unbelief only mild resistance.

In England the steps in this odd evolution in religious thought, from belief to scepticism, can be clearly traced. In the 17th century, the Cambridge Platonists, a small group of clergymen and academics at Cambridge University, complained of what they called the ranting and hypocrisy of the doctrinal disputes between various sects. They proposed to reduce the Christian message to a few relatively simple, relatively reasonable tenets. Christianity, they said, was essentially the practice of reason, the exercise of virtue, and mystical contemplation. Reason and faith were not contradictory, but sympathetic: reason was the way to faith; faith enhanced reason.

Towards the end of the 17th century this rationalist theology was taken up by a larger and more influential group, the Latitudinarians. The members of this group included some of the leading Churchmen of England, among them the eloquent John Tillotson, Archbishop of Canterbury from 1691 to 1694. Like other Latitudinarians, Tillotson vigorously defended the use of reason in reading the Scriptures and denounced what he termed religious "enthusiasm", by which he meant the emotional transports encouraged by revivalist religions. He stressed the ethical purpose of religious instruction: men should reform their conduct; they should be generous, humane and tolerant, and eschew bigotry and fanaticism. The Latitudinarians considered themselves good Christians, but their piety was so moderate that it was hardly distinguishable from general good will.

Six years after England's Glorious Revolution unseated a Catholic monarch, James II, from the throne and re-established the Protestant succession, the intellectual spokesman for that Revolution, John Locke, expanded the Latitudinarian idea. Locke's *Reasonableness of Christianity* encouraged wider tolerance of religious minorities (except atheists, whose word, Locke said, could not be trusted in a court of law, and Roman Catholics, whom he considered agents of a foreign power). He preached modesty in the face of nature's mysteries and held that revelation was an extension of reason. Miracles, he said, were natural occurrences that only seemed supernatural because they lay outside man's comprehension. Similarly, he did not deny that Christianity was true, but he did argue that Christian doctrine could be reduced to a single assertion: that Jesus Christ was the Messiah. Much of

the rest of what Christians were taught to accept as truth was, Locke said, fiction—the invention of superstitious or power-hungry priests.

From here to the position of the deists—that the only proof of God's existence lay in his visible works—was but a short step, and the deists soon took it. But Locke's ideas appealed to orthodox Christians, too, and his reasonable theology pervaded the Church of England throughout the 18th century. Not all of this popularity was based on his religious ideas. Rationalism was associated with the upper classes, as "enthusiasm" was equated with lower-class behaviour—and the Church of England catered by preference to the rich, well-educated and well-born.

The popularity of Locke's rationalism also had political overtones: England longed for religious peace. Although the Glorious Revolution had returned Protestants to the throne, the succession was again thrown into doubt when Queen Anne died in 1714 without direct heirs. Would she be succeeded by her half-brother, the Catholic James, or by her distant German relative, the Protestant George of Hanover? The immediate religious question was answered when George took over the throne and put down a Catholic uprising. But turmoil among the clergy continued over the place of the Church under the new dynasty. It seemed essential, for the sake of political calm, to bring the Church under State control. Thus it was that the Church of England—especially during the period when the great Sir Robert Walpole was principal Minister of State—became politically useful and theologically insignificant.

The device used to subdue the Church was called translation. The career of one Anglican clergyman, Benjamin Hoadly, shows how it worked. It also shows the length to which religious rationalism had gone by the early 18th century. All 26 bishops of the Church of England sat in the House of Lords,

A "PLURALIST" PARSON *stretches over four rich parishes in this 18th-century cartoon satirizing the sad state of the Church in England. Pluralist clerics, appointed by powerful friends, drew several "absentee" incomes—employing poor curates to do the preaching.*

where their votes were sometimes decisive. A clergyman obedient to the government and eloquent in his defence of the royal policies could hope for elevation to one of these bishoprics. With the advancement went improved social standing, increased salary and—in the usual manner of political position—the dispensation of patronage. But an ambitious cleric could not afford to relax, even after he had attained the rank of bishop. Bishoprics varied greatly in desirability, and ordinarily a churchman was assigned one of the least rewarding posts first. Then, if he continued to behave himself and be helpful to his superiors, he was transferred, or translated, to a better post.

In 1715, Benjamin Hoadly, having served the government well, became Bishop of Bangor, a distant Welsh See that carried a modest stipend of £500 a year. But Hoadly never visited his diocese: he was much too busy working for Sir Robert Walpole in London. In 1721 he was rewarded for his work with the bishopric of Hereford. After that, he moved in succession to the bishoprics of Salisbury and Winchester, where he commanded the princely sum of £5,000 a year, together with other desirable perquisites.

Hoadly doubtless earned his keep politically, but his religious beliefs were so tepid that they were criticized even by moderate Latitudinarians. In a celebrated sermon of 1717, he claimed that since Christ had said His kingdom was not of this world, the Church was invisible too. And being invisible, it had no right to exercise its power over worldly matters of any kind. Furthermore, said Hoadly, the Church's requirement of visible proof of orthodoxy—such as the recitation of creeds and the participation in sacraments—was nonsense.

Such words did not signal the end of religion, but they did show that men's relations with God had changed. The traditional Christian doctrine of man's unworthiness was blandly disregarded. Instead, men approached God with gentle awe, with feelings of benevolence and cheerfulness. Joseph Addison's famous hymn published in his periodical, *The Spectator*, is typical of this new attitude:

> *The Spacious Firmament on high*
> *With all the blue Etherial Sky,*
> *And spangled Heav'ns, a Shining Frame*
> *Their great Original proclaim:*
> *Th' unwearied Sun, from Day to Day*
> *Does his Creator's Power display,*
> *And publishes to every Land*
> *The Work of an Almighty Hand.*

Obviously it was not a very demanding sort of religion. The rise of Methodism—with its fervent Christian message and its indefatigable forays into

# PROTESTANTS

```
LUTHERANS        CALVINISTS              ANGLICANS           OTHER SECTS
    |            /       \               /        \          /        \
 Pietists   Huguenots  Presbyterians  Latitudinarians Methodists  Mennonites  Dissenters
                                                                              /  /  \  \
                                                              Congregationalists  Quakers  Baptists  Unitarians
```

LUTHERANS: The first Protestants, followers of Martin Luther, an apostate German monk. Opposed elaborate hierarchy and ritual; favoured the individual's humble, direct communion with God.

PIETISTS: Challenged Lutheran dogma. They emphasized good works, and regarded religion as an emotional rather than an intellectual experience.

CALVINISTS: Strong moralists, they insisted that all personal and public activity, including government, be subordinated to God's will. Believed in predestination. The Puritans of old and New England were Calvinists.

HUGUENOTS: French Calvinists; following bitter persecution, they achieved legal standing in 1802.

PRESBYTERIANS: Scottish Calvinists adhering to the Bible as the arbiter of faith. Emphasized Church government by presbyters, or elders.

ANGLICANS: Englishmen who held both the Catholic belief that the Church's bishops trace their spiritual authority to Christ and the apostles, and the Protestant belief in the Bible as the standard of faith and life.

LATITUDINARIANS: Anglicans who attached little importance to liturgy, Church organization or dogma. Had strong ties to the Cambridge Platonists (*see below*).

METHODISTS: Stressed a methodical organization and a more personal, emotional approach to religion than the Anglicans. Methodism featured itinerant preachers, circuit riders and revival meetings.

MENNONITES: Opposed infant baptism, believing that only those old enough to experience grace should be baptized.

CONGREGATIONALISTS: Believed that each local congregation had its own relationship to God and thus was an autonomous member of a common family

QUAKERS: Held there was no need for a trained priest or formal rites to establish communion between an individual and God.

BAPTISTS: Stressed Bible study and a fundamentalist view of religion. Restricted baptism to those old enough to understand its meaning.

UNITARIANS: Stressed free belief. They held God was one, not a Trinity, that Christ was human, and that salvation came by man's efforts, not God's grace.

# CATHOLICS

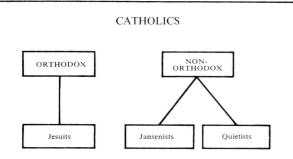

```
ORTHODOX         NON-ORTHODOX
    |             /         \
 Jesuits    Jansenists   Quietists
```

JESUITS: Organized in 1534 by ex-soldier Ignatius Loyola, members of this militant, unyielding Catholic order aroused opposition from Protestants, Catholics and even the Pope himself. In the 18th century the Jesuits were suppressed for a time by the Church and expelled from France, Portugal and Spain.

JANSENISTS: Started by Cornelius Otto Jansen in 1617. Reformed Roman Catholic doctrine by returning to the individualistic ideas of St. Augustine. Jansenists emphasized personal holiness, predestination and the need for divine grace.

QUIETISTS: Believed that man, to perfect himself, must become passive and abandon his soul to God. Held sacraments and confession superfluous. Condemned in 1687 by a papal bull.

# PHILOSOPHERS

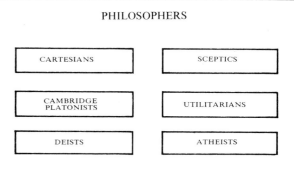

```
CARTESIANS              SCEPTICS
CAMBRIDGE PLATONISTS    UTILITARIANS
DEISTS                  ATHEISTS
```

CARTESIANS: Disciples of Descartes; discarded authoritarianism and argued that only that which is clearly perceived is true.

CAMBRIDGE PLATONISTS: Revived the Platonic theory of ideas, particularly the belief that moral ideas are innate in man.

DEISTS: Argued that the course of nature was sufficient to demonstrate God's existence. Regarded formal religion as superfluous. Their number included Rousseau, Voltaire, Benjamin Franklin, Thomas Jefferson.

SCEPTICS: Denied the ability of man to know all and the capacity of his reason to penetrate everything.

UTILITARIANS: Held that the happiness of the greatest number is the greatest good.

ATHEISTS: Flatly denied God's existence.

a narrow *élite* of educated men and women in the Western world. They especially admired the Roman poet Lucretius, who had equated *religio* with *superstitio*, and called upon men to free themselves from the absurd fear of death. Lucretius appealed to spirits as diverse as the *philosophe* Baron d'Holbach, who believed in the innate goodness of man, and the Prussian monarch Frederick the Great, who spoke of "this damned human race".

In the 18th century, as in ancient times, Epicureanism took two forms. There were those who understood Epicurus's doctrine correctly: the supreme good in life was *ataraxia*, serenity, the absence of pain and disturbing emotions. And then there were others, better known, who treated Epicurean teachings as a licence to indiscriminate self-indulgence. Their motto was "eat, drink, and be merry", a genial, cynical maxim drawn from what was probably the only book in the Bible these latter-day pagans liked—the Book of Ecclesiastes.

One notorious centre for the Epicureanism of excess was the English Court of Charles II after the restoration of the monarchy in 1660. Many Englishmen, undoubtedly weary of the sober restraints imposed on them by the previous ruler, Oliver Cromwell, reacted by going to the opposite extreme. They affected obscene speech, indulged their lusts, ridiculed marital fidelity and blasphemed the sacred. In France a similar reaction to the monotonous Court life in the last years of Louis XIV produced a similar group during the regency of his successor, the Duc d'Orléans. The Regent, intelligent and debauched, loved wine and women and easily found congenial company in the pursuit of both.

By far the most interesting mind among the devotees of pagan pleasure was a French aristocrat, the Seigneur de Saint-Evremond. During the reign of Louis XIV, Saint-Evremond had served with distinction in the army, but he spent the second half of his life, for political reasons, living idly and happily in exile. A man of letters and elegant wit, Saint-Evremond wrote brilliant essays on literature and drama and kept up an equally brilliant correspondence with his friends, one of whom was the celebrated courtesan Ninon de Lenclos, mistress to some of the most distinguished men of France. In all things, in his writings as in his conduct, Saint-Evremond was a gourmet of life: he sought pleasure and found it. But he also believed in moderation and tolerance: "An imperfect enjoyment is attended with Regret; a surfeit of Pleasure with Disgust; there's a certain nick of time, a certain medium to be observ'd, with which few people are acquainted. We must enjoy the presènt Pleasures, without impairing the future".

Not surprisingly, in view of this general outlook, Saint-Evremond, his associates and his spiritual kinsmen had little use for Christianity. They thought it gloomy, hostile to life and altogether absurd. It became their favourite target of scurrility. They asked mocking questions, often in the worst of taste—about the chastity of the Virgin, the real motives of Christian saints, and the gulf between Christian precepts and Christian conduct. Since blasphemy was illegal, and since in many countries the censors were powerful clergymen, most of this scurrilous sacrilege was never printed. Irreligious poems were learned by heart and recited behind closed doors, or circulated in manuscript from hand to hand.

Much of this impiety was a social game, but sometimes it wore serious faces too, the faces of scholarship and philosophy. Ever since the early days of Christianity, intelligent believers had been embarrassed by the conflicting accounts of the Creation and other sacred events, and by the obscurity of many Scriptural passages. Indeed, one reason for the rise of the authoritarian Catholic Church had been just this profusion of contradictory and often incomprehensible Biblical writings: God sometimes spoke in riddles that only trained minds could solve and in contradictions that only a firm authority could reconcile.

Down through the centuries, Churchmen had wrestled with the precise meaning of certain passages and argued over the authenticity of the numerous versions of saints' lives. But until the Renaissance no one, not even the most learned Christians, thought to question extraordinary tales of visions and miraculous happenings. Then, with the rise of humanism, scepticism crept in and scholars began to weed out forgeries and purify the text of the Scriptures. By the 17th century a small army of pious scholars, most prominently Flemish Jesuits and French Benedictines, was applying severe tests to religious documents of all sorts—finally even to the Bible itself.

But all this activity was merely meant to purify the faith, to rid it of false accretions. A more devastating sort of criticism came in the same century from philosophers like Thomas Hobbes and Baruch Spinoza. Working outside the mainstream of society and regarded almost universally as dangerous atheists, Hobbes and Spinoza treated the Bible as a book like any other book. By the end of the 17th century, a few scholars, though still only a very few, agreed with them. They were in accord, for instance, that Moses could not have been the sole author of the first five books of the Old Testament, as tradition claimed, since the last of these describes his death.

By the 18th century this sort of analysis, stripping the Bible of its holy mystery, was a commonplace among liberal theologians, especially in the Protestant faiths. And it had become so, in large part, through the propaganda activities of the deists. Deism was a philosophy to which rational and educated men found it easy to give assent. It had a large and impressive following in England,

where it started; in France, where it had its greatest success; in certain German States and in the American colonies. French *philosophes* as different as Voltaire and Jean Jacques Rousseau were deists, and so were such Americans as Thomas Jefferson and Benjamin Franklin.

Although sceptics from the left and philosophical Christians from the right assailed the movement as shallow, deism was a sensible philosophy and, as Goethe observed towards the end of the 18th century, a natural sort of religious philosophy for most educated men to adopt.

A movement so widespread and varied is not easy to define. Almost a century ago, the English literary historian Leslie Stephen divided deism into two aspects, critical and constructive. While this division was never absolute—most deists were both critical and constructive—it offers a useful point from which to start.

Critical deism was concerned with attacking and downgrading conventional Christianity. It drew its ammunition from the Biblical scholarship of its own time, and from the scepticism about miracles and clerical morality that had been circulating since the Renaissance. John Toland, the first full-fledged critical deist, argued in his *Christianity Not Mysterious*, published in 1696, that God had given man a religion worthy of him—a reasonable religion, for man was capable of reason. Therefore all the mysteries in Christianity must be later interpolations inserted by power-hungry priests.

Toland's followers took this line even further. Anthony Collins, in *A Discourse of the Grounds and Reasons of the Christian Religion*, published in 1724, asked men to read the Bible as they would any other great book. He denied that the prophecies of the Old Testament had really come true, although theologians for centuries had rested part of their case for the authenticity of Christianity on the argument that events foretold by Jewish

SACRED OATHS AT SWORD-POINT *were exacted during rites at Free-masons' lodges, major meeting places for intellectuals in the 18th century (members included Voltaire and Frederick the Great). Other candidates, under shrouds, await their turns on the left.*

prophets in the Old Testament had been fulfilled in the New. According to Collins, this argument rested on the twisting of words and extravagant allegorical explanations of arcana and obscure tales —on explanations, in other words, that could be made to explain anything at all.

Thomas Woolston's scandalous *Six Discourses on the Miracles of Our Savior*, published between 1727 and 1729, followed the same line, but was even more extreme in tone. Woolston claimed that the central miracle of the Christian faith, the Resurrection of Christ, was "the most notorious and monstrous Imposture, that ever was put upon mankind". Furthermore, he said, all miracles were inspired by the devil, and so could scarcely be taken as proof of the miracle-worker's divinity. The deists were nothing if not bold.

These arguments, and others like them, spread across Europe in numerous editions, in translation and in paraphrase, but above all in the voluminous writings of Voltaire, who borrowed the arguments of the English deists but gave them a lightness of tone and an irresistible wit which the earnest and intense English polemics never attained. Probably Voltaire became a deist fairly early in life—he was certainly one by the 1720's, when he was still in his thirties. But he did not publish much deist propaganda until he was old, rich, famous and relatively safe from prosecution. Then, in his seventies, living in luxury in his château at Ferney, he began to pour out deist tracts in tireless profusion. The most famous of them is his *Philosophical Dictionary*, first published anonymously in 1764, and often reissued and enlarged.

Although the *Dictionary* contains articles on literature, on the theory of knowledge and on ethics, about three-quarters of it is devoted to deist propaganda. All the familiar deist arguments tumble forth: the only valuable elements in Christianity are those that are identical with the teachings of the great philosophers; all else is nonsense. The Jews of the Bible, the so-called "Chosen People", were primitive peasants with little culture and bad morals, thieves and murderers. The Church

39

Fathers were little better; they were ignorant, superstitious, power-hungry, quarrelsome men. The Bible, both the Old and New Testaments, was a collection of incoherent maxims and improbable stories, celebrating crimes and absurdities. The history of Christianity was a history of squabbles over mere words, of incitements to crime and cruelty and war. "Theology amuses me", wrote Voltaire in the 1760's, when he was completing the *Dictionary*. "There we find man's insanity in all its plenitude." It was a grim, bellicose amusement, designed to destroy a faith that Voltaire thought unworthy of man.

On the constructive side, the deists spelt out what they believed to be a more suitable conception of God. For this they drew upon a body of philosophical writings going back to Cicero and the ancient Greek Stoics, who believed that God was manifest in all the workings of nature, but that explaining His universe was less important than adjusting oneself to it. The deists did not deny the existence of a God: the whole universe, with its beauty, its vastness, its intricate design, testified to His presence and His superb skill. But the deist God was like a great Watchmaker, or—as some of the deists liked to say—a great Mathematician; He had created the world, given it laws to run by, and then had withdrawn. Thereafter, the world, following His immutable laws, ran itself.

From this conception of God it followed, first of all, that miracles, as such, were impossible. A miracle, as sceptic David Hume put it, was a "violation of the laws of nature". To talk of miracles, the deists said, to talk of divine intervention in the natural course of events, was to cast a reflection of God: the Deity, they said, had not botched the job of creating the universe and did not need to intervene to set things straight.

Secondly, the deist conception of God implied that there were universal moral laws which all reasonable men could discover, and that the ethical teachings of all the great philosophers—Eastern or Western, Christian or pagan—converged on the same moral questions. They all taught decency, generosity, honesty and uprightness—and these were all that a man needed to guide him through life. Man should be worshipful, the deists said: the world was so marvellous a place that an attitude of awe was proper. But he needed no churches, no prayers, no saints, no communion, no priests for this act of worship. All he needed was clarity of thought.

This led to the third tenet of deism: rationalism. Man found religious truth, the deists said, by means of his powers of reason. Not that reason would make everything knowable: there was much that would always remain mysterious to man. But all other methods of knowing—divine inspiration, clerical authority, the teachings of the Bible or the Church Fathers—were sure roads to ignorance. Only reason—and on this point all the deists, whatever their divergences, were agreed—only reason led to religious knowledge.

It is easy to see why deism was so popular in the age of Enlightenment, but it is also easy to see why it led to even more radical views. Philosophically it was an unstable compound of belief and disbelief. It denied supernatural intervention in the affairs of the universe, but it affirmed the supernatural existence of God—and its arguments for both positions were based on reason. By the middle of the 18th century, using the same device of reason, aggressive thinkers were beginning to grow sceptical of the very existence of God. They could do without even the deists' God. Thus, moving from a fragile belief to a belligerent disbelief, 18th-century intellectuals progressed finally to a disdainful unbelief that abandoned Christianity entirely and substituted a good society of men on earth for the kingdom of God in heaven.

FRENCHWOMEN *on promenade banter with their escorts, practising what a contemporary Englishman called "the art of society and conversation".*

# THE CAPTIVATING RULERS
# OF FRANCE

Rarely in history have women ruled a nation so completely as they did France during the 18th century. "Everything depends on her", said Rousseau of the woman of his time; "nothing is done except by her or for her." Women assumed this power by default of Louis XV's pleasure-seeking Court and an aristocracy which was too dissolute to pay attention to the real activity of the moment: the ferment of ideas stirring all Europe. By controlling the nation's intellectual life as well as its affairs of State, aristocratic women cast France in their own image—exquisite, quick-witted, gay and deceptive. No society was ever more delightful—or cultivated so brilliantly the seeds of its own destruction.

AWAKING LATE, *a lady of fashion, assisted by maids who pull back the bed curtains and present her slippers, prepares to greet another day in which each simple occasion will be filled with elaborate formality and manners.*

AT HER TOILETTE, *always a protracted rite, a stylish lady reads a treatise on coiffure while her elegant visitor flirts with the maid and a cat toys with a ribbon. Small animals—dogs, monkeys, parrots—were popular playthings.*

# ELEGANCE IN THE PURSUIT OF PLEASURE

Private life for a woman of French society was an elaborate ceremonial from the moment she awoke until the small hours of each day. Her *toilette* was a public affair at which friends, lovers, hairdressers, husbands, abbés and others gathered to exchange new rumours, or to give old rumours new sparkle by a graceful turn of phrase. Marriage scarcely interfered with a woman's freedom to amuse herself; "a husband who would wish to have sole possession of his wife", Montesquieu said, "would be regarded as a disturber of public happiness". Marital separation required only that a wife arrange for the man to slap her before two witnesses. This, and every other social situation, she met with style and elegance. Imitation of the aristocratic Frenchwoman's exquisite manners soon became the hopeless goal of all fashionable Europe.

A GAME OF WHIST *illustrates the ladies' obsession with gambling. One duchess, called to the deathbed of a friend, took cards, table and companions to the scene so that play—and the accompanying gossip—would not be interrupted.*

A PROMENADE on a boulevard displays women to admiring onlookers. This delicate exercise had become such a fashion that parks and gardens reserved special days and hours for the ritual. Long canes were standard equipment.

A MUSIC LESSON in the afternoon, like every other activity, finds a gentleman in the audience. The harp was a favoured instrument: it presented madame with the opportunity to appear graceful and talented simultaneously.

CONVERSATION consumes two ladies. Talk was an art, "a gay dialogue in which each listens but little, yet speaks . . . in a rapid, prompt, and vivacious manner". At large gatherings even the King had to shout to be heard.

COURTSHIP followed a pattern as predictable as a brocade's: by formula, a swain woos beside a statue of Cupid, the lady is arch, and her mother, hidden in the shrubbery, listens to detect honest intentions amid the platitudes. 43

MADAME DE POMPADOUR *appears in this portrait by François Boucher against an interior stamped by her exquisite rococo taste. A talented musician, singer, actress, painter, etcher and engraver, she was among the leading patrons of the arts.*

# THE INFLUENTIAL LADIES OF THE COURT

At Versailles, the main job of 2,000 courtiers was to keep Louis XV from being bored. He bored easily. After a few years of marriage he took up with a series of women, including three sisters. The woman who pleased the King controlled the court, but satisfying Louis's precarious temper demanded prodigious skills. Madame de Pompadour (*above*) had all the requirements: talent, taste and an un-

erring touch (except when her personal pique against Frederick the Great helped to spark a disastrous war with Prussia). Pompadour might change her dress every hour, yet her dynamic intelligence won the approval of a generation of artists and intellectuals. She ruled the ruler for 20 years as his official mistress, but her beauty faded. When she died, it was said, the King wept exactly two tears.

A BRILLIANT BALL *honouring the Dauphin's marriage was where the King and Pompadour met. He was one of eight men dressed as yew trees (left). As he strolled past, she dropped her handkerchief, starting the great affair.*

THE PLEASURES OF ROMANCE *are sampled by this foursome as they linger after dinner to enjoy with studied amusement, the reading aloud of a love letter. Such entertainments were as much a part of Court life as balls or theatricals.*

# INTELLECTUAL FERMENT IN THE SALONS OF PARIS

As new ideas demanding an audience arose in France, remarkable women established salons in their houses to substitute for a negligent Court. Salons were so influential that Catherine the Great of Russia found it advisable to post a salaried commissioner at the Monday and Wednesday dinners of Madame Geoffrin, the lace-capped lady seated third from the right.

Her salon was the most eminent of all; she was surrounded, Denis Diderot said, "by all that are of any consequence, whether in the capital or at Court". The gentlemen shown here listening to a reading by the actor Lekain were typical: among them are Jean Jacques Rousseau, Diderot and the great mathematician, Jean Le Rond d'Alembert. Under the knowing eyes of "drawing room despots" like Madame Geoffrin, aristocrats and men of letters mingled, each polishing the flaws of the others until the resulting product represented the essence of civilization. Conversation was perfected to an art in salons, and the French language was so meticulously honed that it became the world's precision instrument of diplomacy.

DISTRACTED THEATRE-GOERS *in a private box find their attention diverted from the opera to a curtsying actress. "The whole world [was] dreaming theatre", wrote a later commentator, "from one end of France to the other."*

A FEMME FATALE, *Sophie Arnould of the Opéra-Comique, was an actress, singer and wit. When weary of her titled lover, she dispatched to his wife everything he had given to her: jewels, coach and children.*

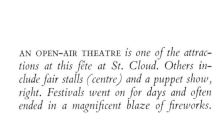

AN OPEN-AIR THEATRE *is one of the attractions at this fête at St. Cloud. Others include fair stalls (centre) and a puppet show, right. Festivals went on for days and often ended in a magnificent blaze of fireworks.*

# THEATRE: THE ULTIMATE EXTRAVAGANCE

Theatrical entertainment had to assume extravagant proportions to outdo the scale of society's ordinary pleasures—and it did so. The theatre, though condemned by the Church, was everybody's passion, and 18th-century comedy reflected the era's delight in repartee, gaiety and intrigue. Leading actresses were excommunicated, but were admired by society and made welcome at Versailles. ("We delight to live with them, and object to be buried with them", observed Voltaire.) Royalty and aristocracy joined professionals in lavish private productions. Even the king occasionally crossed a stage.

# CHILDREN: LONELY LITTLE GROWN-UPS

One of the areas in which the mannered society of 18th-century France made its strongest impact was in the way the upper classes treated children. From the time that they were babies, boys and girls were dressed as adults, and treated impersonally like pretty toys. They scarcely ever saw their parents. A typical little girl of the nobility would be weaned by a wet nurse, then handed over to a governess to be taught manners. At 5 she would be put in a convent, and at 15 taken out and pushed into a desirable marriage. Boys, too, were kept distant from their parents. "The most useful of all arts, that of making men, is forgotten", Rousseau wrote.

Rousseau helped to bring about a change. When he suggested that a child should be given the opportunity to develop his natural gifts unhampered and shielded from the corruption of the day, he found many fashionable mothers supporting him. By such reasonable rebellion against one element of the society they had created, women encouraged rebellion against their whole society—and helped to lead, some say, to its end in the French Revolution.

LIKE MINIATURE ADULTS, *two overdressed children pay formal respects to their mother in the day's only visit. The girl's hoop skirt extends below a whalebone corset, which she learned to wear as soon as she could walk.*

A CHANGE IN ATTITUDE *towards children is shown in this picture of a mother holding her infant, while the father and governess look on. But the change came slowly; children still could not engage in rough play.*

# 3

# IN SEARCH OF AN IDEAL SOCIETY

Immanuel Kant once observed that while his age was an age of enlightenment, it was not an enlightened age. It was an age whose literary spokesmen preached the virtues of reason and good sense and humane regard for one's fellow man. But it was not an age that had achieved these virtues. To the most aggressive thinkers of the 18th century, the rationality of their Christian friends was not rational enough, the broadminded policies of their Statesmen needed to be carried further. They wanted society to be wholly secular and governments to be devoted wholly to the general welfare. As the age progressed, the views of these men became increasingly radical.

The first generation of *philosophes*, men like Montesquieu and Voltaire, were deists. So were some of their younger contemporaries, like Rousseau. Deism, in fact, continued to be popular right through the 18th century. Around the middle of the century, however, two other philosophies gained followers. One was the scepticism of David Hume, the other was the atheism of a group of *philosophes* whose central figure was the wealthy expatriate German nobleman, Baron d'Holbach.

Hume was in many ways typical of the civilized men of his day; he was untypical only in his enormous intellectual daring. Born in Scotland in 1711 into dour Scottish Presbyterian surroundings, he had reasoned himself out of his religious faith and laid the groundwork for his sceptical philosophy before he was out of his teens. At 29 he published the first of his masterpieces, *A Treatise of Human Nature*. The book was so abstract in thought and difficult in language that few people understood it; in Hume's own words, it "fell deadborn from the press". Later, acting as his own popularizer, he presented the main arguments of the *Treatise* in a more readable form.

Philosophy was only one of Hume's literary activities. Between 1754 and 1762 he published, in instalments, a *History of England* that became the standard work in its field and made him rich. During the same period he also published a quantity of essays on various subjects, a few trivial, many important. In one of them, "The Populousness of Ancient Nations", he laid the foundations for modern demography—the scientific study of population statistics. Several others anticipated the economic ideas of his friend Adam Smith, the great exponent of free trade: the basis of wealth was not money, said Hume, but men; it was the labour force that accounted for "all real power and riches". And in still others he disagreed with political theorists like Locke, who held that political institutions arose as a result of social contracts between men. Not so, said Hume, and offered instead an anthropological account of their rise.

Two of Hume's works in particular stirred up angry comment and rebuttal. One was his essay "The Natural History of Religion", which suggested that all religious sentiments grew out of two quite human emotions, hope and fear—especially fear. Even the title of this essay was radical. Few men in the middle of the 18th century would have willingly conceded that religion had a natural history, like any other worldly institution.

The second of the two controversial works, *Dialogues concerning Natural Religion*, was a witty rejection of both the Christian and deist theories of the nature of religious truth. The *Dialogues* has three speakers: a philosopher, a believer and a sceptic. The philosopher holds that God exists because the workings of nature are too marvellous to be the product of chance; they must have been created by some superior intelligence. The "reasonableness" of this explanation shocks the believer but it leaves the sceptic unconvinced. Why, he asks, should the role of intelligence be so exalted? "What peculiar privilege has this little agitation of the brain called thought, that we must make it the model of the whole universe?".

Except for his feelings about Christianity, Hume was an amiable, moderate man, and his very moderation made him more formidable. He claimed that men could be absolutely certain about truth in only one field: mathematics. "Two plus two equals four" was true without qualification, in all times and all places, because numerical relations were "relations of ideas". In all other relations truth depended on "matters of fact"—and facts were always open to question since they concerned things, not ideas. Thus the statement "Caesar died in bed" might be right or wrong, depending on the evidence collected for it—and men would have to be content with probability, since absolute certainty was impossible.

These distinctions may sound like philosophical hair-splitting, but Hume's contemporaries found them deeply disturbing. In undermining absolute truth, he destroyed the reassurance of dogma and invited men to live with perpetual uncertainty, a condition few men can stand. Unlike some earlier sceptics, however, Hume did not carry his scepticism to extremes. The ancient Greek philosopher Pyrrho, doubting every sense perception, had recommended complete detachment and indifference to all worldly things. But Hume thought it was enough for a man to be a sceptic in the isolation of his study. When he came out of his study, his natural passions and common sense should lead him back to a cheerful involvement in the uncertainties of everyday life.

Despite this moderation, Hume's scepticism, demanding and austere, had few followers. Atheism, the other rival to deism, fared rather better. Its roots, too, were in ancient Greek philosophy. To certain Greek philosophers the basic unit of the universe was the atom: all things were composed of masses of atoms, all thoughts and sensations derived from atomic interaction. Thus, nothing existed but matter. Water was made of water atoms, round and smooth; iron was made of iron atoms, jagged and rough; and the soul was made of soul atoms, round and smooth and especially mobile. In the 17th century, when scientific discoveries revived interest in such theories, atomism gained new currency. And in the 18th century it became incorporated into a materialist philosophy which accounted for the universe without recourse to God.

One of the most persuasive statements of this philosophy was a notorious little book, *Man a Machine*, written and published in 1747 by Julien Offroy de la Mettrie. La Mettrie was a physician who had studied under one of the greatest medical scientists of his day, the Dutch doctor Hermann Boerhaave. Consequently his philosophical studies were coloured by what he knew about biology. He believed, for instance, that all mental activity—both mood and thought—derived from physical activity. Thus, the idea of a soul was unnecessary.

La Mettrie was willing to concede that a Supreme Being might exist, but he thought that His existence was of theoretical interest only. He did not need to be worshipped, and He certainly did not need to be considered a source of moral law. Man made such laws for himself, basing them on his own physical and psychological needs: what was good for man was right. Accordingly, La Mettrie said that pleasure-seeking was morally sound and recommended it as "preventive medicine" for pain. "Doctor, cure thyself!" he quoted wryly, and practising what he preached, stifled his own attacks of melancholy with "the Opera, Concerts, the Theatre, Dinner, Dances and even Marionettes".

La Mettrie may sometimes have talked and acted like a libertine, but he could behave with decency, too. Indeed, he had some remarkably enlightened ideas about the treatment of criminals, whose actions, he said, were often the result of a disordered machine—a view curiously close to the modern one. Unfortunately, La Mettrie's theories—and his lack of tact—offended many people. Forced to flee first Paris, then Holland, he settled finally in Prussia at the invitation of Frederick the Great, one of the great patrons of the *philosophes*. In Prussia, La Mettrie continued to pour out materialist propaganda and search out pleasure as an antidote to pain. He died suddenly in 1751, shortly after eating large helpings of paté of pheasant with truffles, at a dinner party given by one of his patients. For once, said Voltaire, the patient had killed the doctor.

Luckily for the materialist cause, other atheists were more abstemious. In the same decade that La Mettrie died, the Baron d'Holbach, born in the German Palatinate but a resident of Paris for most of his life, began to interest himself in philosophy. Holbach was a scientist, the author of some 400 articles, largely on chemistry and mineralogy, in Diderot's *Encyclopédie*. He was a clear if rather rigid thinker who "paraded his ideas" (as some critics have put it) with the orderliness of a German military mind.

A generous and systematic host, Holbach entertained regularly in his house in Paris and his country house near by. His dinner parties were symposiums for radical men of letters. Hume, who often dined at Holbach's when he was assigned to the British Embassy in Paris, expressed his amazement at finding himself surrounded by doctrinaire atheists. Indeed, while the dinner company was not exclusively atheist, its roster reads like an intellectual *Who's Who* of the age: Laurence Sterne, Horace Walpole and Adam Smith from Britain; Cesare Bonesana, marchese di Beccaria, the great legal reformer from Milan; Benjamin Franklin from the New World—and Diderot, always Diderot, Holbach's great friend and often his silent collaborator.

By the 1760's, after sampling several philosophies, Holbach had settled into a consistently atheistic point of view and had begun to proselytize for it. With the help of his literary friends he ran a veritable propaganda factory, turning out a host of anonymous and pseudonymous books and pamphlets. Some were printed clandestinely in France, others were printed in Holland, where a Protestant government was more tolerant of religious radicals. The most outrageous of them were provided with innocuous title pages to disguise their contents.

Of all this copious output, the most important work was Holbach's own *System of Nature*. It was published in 1770 over the name of Mirabaud, a former secretary of the French Academy who had been obligingly dead for 10 years. The *System of Nature* begins with the statement that man is unhappy because he is ignorant of nature, and goes on to say that this ignorance is the mother of religion. Religion, in turn, spawns further ignorance, since self-serving clergymen—and also wicked rulers—prefer to keep men spiritually in the dark.

Actually, continues Holbach, there is no God; there is nothing but nature. And just as man's emotions derive from nature, so should his moral principles. Mortality can be sound only if it is based on a comprehension of natural order and disregards fables about miracles, incarnations, trinities and such. Those who say that atheists are immoral are not merely mistaken, he writes, they pervert the truth. It is belief, not non-belief, that inspires crime and invents persecutions for "heretics", "apostates" and "witches". Only a society of atheists, concludes Holbach, has any hope of being moral.

A radical in religion, Holbach was also a radical in politics. Indeed, all the *philosophes* from Montesquieu to Kant agreed that the two subjects that needed discussion most—and got it least—were religion and politics. And in political thought, as in religion, they were fundamentally of one mind. The ideal society was a secular society: the subjects of a State should obey its laws for political and legal reasons, not on religious or tribal grounds. The *philosophes* all agreed, too, on the right to dissent, the right to free speech for all reasonable men, an end to arbitrary government, an end to cruel treatment of accused persons, an end to torture as an instrument of interrogation or punishment. In short, men of the Enlightenment everywhere were,

in the broad sense of the word, political liberals.

But despite the general liberality of their sentiments, there were points on which the *philosophes* disagreed. Living under widely different political conditions, and being tough-minded realists, they tailored their individual political ideas to the conditions they knew best. In England, where the Glorious Revolution of 1688 had curbed the power of the king and strengthened the power of Parliament, *philosophes* were too contented to be radicals. Hume was interested in political theory and analysed the foundations of government; Gibbon was interested in the conduct of political affairs, and, in his celebrated history of the Roman Empire, exposed the cant and tricks of politicians. But neither man had any fundamental complaint against the British constitutional system.

Only John Wilkes, with his pamphleteering on behalf of Parliamentary reforms, managed to arouse the British public to acts of political protest—although nothing came of them until more than half a century later.

Spain was even less touched by political radicalism than England, for only the most innocuous of the *philosophes*' ideas were permitted to reach Spanish readers. As for the Italian States, there the radical political ideas never spread much beyond the circles of intellectuals. Beccaria, the Milanese legal reformer, and other Italian reformers met in discussion clubs modelled on those of their English counterparts and published moralizing weekly journals in imitation of Addison and Steele's famous *Spectator*. Sometimes they even sought the ear of their princes—and sometimes, though not usually, they got it.

In Germany the spread of political radicalism was complicated by the fact that practically all of the 300-odd sovereign German States had traditional autocratic governments; political discussion was either discouraged or forbidden outright. Even in

Prussia, where Frederick the Great lionized visiting *philosophes*, people were not encouraged to criticize the existing Establishment. Free speech in Prussia, in the bitter opinion of the German author Gotthold Lessing, amounted to little more than permission to make anticlerical jokes. "Argue as much as you like," Kant urged his readers, "but obey."

It was in France, where the balance between the Enlightenment and the Establishment was relatively even, that political liberalism of various stripes found its most outspoken and eloquent expression. Indeed, the arguments between individual *philosophes* were almost as lively as the argument between *philosophes* and the forces of orthodoxy. France in the 18th century was deeply divided over the question of political authority. Some people sided with the king and his ministers, who claimed that only the king could make laws and that his will was irrevocable. Some sided with the *parlements*, the great French law courts dominated by the aristocracy, who claimed that the courts had the right to examine laws and reject any they did not like. Both sides had plausible arguments, and Frenchmen of every philosophical persuasion came to the aid of both, creating a dense tangle of political thought. Nowhere is this variety more brilliantly illuminated than in the writings of three men—one a nobleman, one a bourgeois and one a man from the artisan class.

The nobleman was Charles Louis de Secondat, Baron de la Brède et de Montesquieu, born in 1689 at La Brède, near Bordeaux. As a young man Montesquieu wrote widely on a variety of subjects—a eulogy of Cicero, a satire on European society, *The Persian Letters*, and an essay on the reasons for ancient Rome's grandeur and decline. He also assembled a vast library on history, theology, travel and law. Out of his researches into these subjects came his masterpiece, *The Spirit of the Laws,*

## THE WIT OF VOLTAIRE

In general, the art of government consists in taking as much money as possible from one class of citizens to give it to the other.

Marriage is the only adventure open to the cowardly.

I have never made but one prayer to God, a very short one: "O Lord, make my enemies ridiculous". And God granted it.

Self-love never dies.

The gloomy Englishman, even in his loves, always wants to reason. We are more reasonable in France.

If God did not exist, it would be necessary to invent him.

Men use thought only to justify their wrongdoing, and employ speech only to conceal their thoughts.

It is said that God is always on the side of the big battalions.

All the reasoning of men is not worth one sentiment of women.

To stop criticism they say one must die.

a study of governments which he published, after many years of labour, seven years before his death.

As readers have complained for two centuries, *The Spirit of the Laws* is a sprawling compilation of material assembled indiscriminately from ancient texts, contemporary travellers and Montesquieu's own observations. It has little shape and less organization. Some chapters are little more than a sentence long; others are sizeable essays. But underneath this disorder there is a powerful analytical mind. Montesquieu postulated a "spirit" behind governments that supports them and on occasion causes their downfall. The spirit behind monarchies was "honour"—the ingrained sense of status and responsibility of a working nobility. The spirit behind republics was "virtue"—a sense of civic consciousness. And the spirit behind despotisms was fear. When these supporting principles weakened, the government weakened with them.

In addition, Montesquieu argued, governments are shaped by their physical environment. Climate profoundly influences behaviour and thus the contours of society. "I have attended the opera in England and in Italy," he wrote, and "... saw the same pieces with the same performers; and yet the same music produces very different effects on the two nations: one is so cold, so phlegmatic, the other so lively, excited, that it is almost incredible." England's wet and windy weather, he added, encouraged suicide, while the Mediterranean sun led men to love sensuality for its own sake. And severe northern climates, like Russia's, produced insensibility to pain: "You must flay a Muscovite alive to make him wince". These notions may sound a little naïve, but in fact they were the first step towards the science of sociology.

The goal of *The Spirit of the Laws*, for all its tenuous logic, was freedom. Montesquieu believed that despotism was always bad, and that men should strive to avoid it or prevent its growth. He thought he had discovered one sure means of accomplishing this, and it lay within the British constitution. Montesquieu thought that the British subject's sense of liberty—his feeling of safety and security—sprang from the separation of the government's powers into three parts. The king held executive power only, he said, while Parliament alone could make laws; and the judiciary functioned independently of them both. He buttressed his argument by observing that the power of monarchs had traditionally been held in check by political forces which occupied a place between a king and his common subjects—notably by a working aristocracy.

Montesquieu's views were criticized in his time and have been criticized ever since. Actually, the British government was not divided into three equal, independent parts. The king depended on Parliament for money to run the government, since Parliament alone had the right to levy taxes. Also, the two legislative houses, the House of Commons and particularly the House of Lords, frequently performed judicial functions. In fact, during the very years Montesquieu wrote, the British system of government was in the process of evolution. The House of Commons especially was expanding its influence, and was beginning to establish the principle that the functions of the executive branch —especially the policies and personnel of the Cabinet—were subject to Parliamentary approval.

Montesquieu's case was further damaged by a suspicion among the more radical of the French *philosophes* that his defence of a strong aristocracy was actually a screen behind which the French nobility could continue to exercise its privileges. Their suspicions were not groundless. In the second half of the 18th century, members of the French *parlements* often quoted Montesquieu's works in defence of such traditional aristocratic privileges as

tax exemption. But Montesquieu himself was no aristocratic ideologist masquerading as a liberal. He believed passionately in liberty for all men, not just aristocrats. He condemned the imposition of the death penalty on the testimony of a single witness, and suggested that the severity of punishment be scaled to the degree of the crime. He denounced the use of informers or torture to extract evidence and called for the elimination of all cruel forms of punishment. He ridiculed calling witchcraft a crime, and held that accusations of sorcery and treason ought to be treated with the utmost scepticism. He carefully distinguished treasonable acts (which the law may punish), from treasonable thoughts (which it may not) and treasonable words (which may not be judged treasonable unless connected with treasonable acts).

All the *philosophes* could agree on the noble and humane legal philosophy embodied in *The Spirit of the Laws*. But Voltaire, although he approved of Montesquieu's liberalism, was highly critical of his belief in a strong aristocracy. Voltaire, for all his middle-class origins, was a royalist. He was convinced that the kind of reforms France needed would never come through the crusty *parlements*, whose aristocratic members confused their own interests with those of the State. Such changes, he thought, could only come through the king. Properly advised by informed ministers, the king could rise above personal concerns to order what was good for the State.

Voltaire was not so much an advocate of "enlightened despotism"—of an autocratic but benevolent monarch—as he was of political pragmatism. He argued that the traditions, culture and historical circumstances of each country were different, and that these differences should be taken into account. Thus he admired equally England's strong House of Commons, the commercial aristocracy of the Netherlands, Geneva's liberal republicanism, and

Frederick the Great's autocratic rule over poverty-stricken and ill-educated Prussia. Along with other *philosophes* he was a champion of free speech, a free press and civil liberties, and he thought that in France these were much more likely to be achieved under a strong king, well advised, than under the self-serving *parlements*.

In the 1760's Voltaire underlined these convictions by intervening in several celebrated legal cases in which he saw injustice at work. One involved an elderly Huguenot merchant named Jean Calas, who had been accused of murdering his son—supposedly in a rage over the son's alleged plan to convert to Catholicism. Calas had been tortured and cruelly executed; all four of his limbs had been broken in two places, then he had been strangled, and then burned at the stake. To the end, he had maintained his innocence. At first, Voltaire treated the case simply as a confirmation of his contempt for all Christians: if Calas was innocent, his death was an indictment of his Catholic executioners; if he was guilty, it demonstrated the fanaticism of Protestants. But soon Voltaire saw the case as more than religious propaganda: he wanted to find the truth. Before long, he became convinced that Jean Calas had been the victim of a judicial murder, and set out to rehabilitate his memory. He engaged lawyers to search out new evidence and importune the authorities. He solicited funds to help in the care of the destitute Calas family. He wrote moving accounts of the case and mounted a campaign to reform the French legal system. Finally, three years after the execution, the name of Jean Calas was cleared.

Although Voltaire spoke out boldly against such individual transgressions of liberty, there was one subject on which he—and all the other *philosophes*—wavered: the treatment of the masses. The lower orders of society were for the most part illiterate, or if literate, barely able to write their names. They

CHINESE INFLUENCE *in Europe reached a peak during the 18th century in such manufactures as this British "China" porcelain vase. The fad for "chinoiserie" was everywhere: homes were adorned with Chinese wallpaper and furnishings, ladies carried Chinese parasols, and gentlemen studied Chinese philosophy.*

lived in extreme want, in filth and with little hope, burdened down by disease and economic exploitation. Too irrational to govern themselves, too subject to their passions to be good citizens, they had to be controlled by fear. At this point the interests of religion and politics converged. Religious fear —the fear of hell and eternal damnation—the *philosophes* suggested was being used as an instrument of social control. Seeing this, but thinking it unreasonable to ask a social conscience of men and women scarcely able to exercise a private conscience, most *philosophes* were content to apply Edward Gibbon's observation about ancient Rome to their own time: "The various modes of worship which prevailed in the Roman world", Gibbon wrote, "were all considered by the people as equally true; by the philosophers as equally false; and by the magistrates as equally useful".

But even though the realities of 18th-century life encouraged such policies, the *philosophes* did not think them ideal. Few of them had any theories of progress, but all of them were hopeful that some day reason would win over superstition, and truth over ignorance. Thus, Voltaire wavered. He could speak of the people as "a ferocious and blind monster" and claim that he had "never pretended to enlighten shoemakers and servants; that was the job of the apostles". At the same time, he could distinguish between the propertyless masses and self-respecting artisans. The former, he said, will always spend their time going from the Mass to the tavern and back, because there is singing in both places. But craftsmen and shopkeepers have learned to think, and like to read, and are different. "All is not lost", he wrote, "when one puts the people in a condition to see it has intelligence. On the contrary, all is lost when you treat it like a herd of cattle, for sooner or later it will gore you with its horns."

To many of the *philosophes*, the key to this in-

telligence was education. All men were by nature capable of thought, but had been spoiled and perverted by kings and priests. Education would free man from this bondage. Implicit in this was a criticism of society itself, and the most famous of the social critics was Jean Jacques Rousseau. But Rousseau was not alone. His attacks upon the artificiality of the age, the insincerity, the empty politeness, the desiccation of love and public spirit, were part of a larger sentiment. The *philosophes* were disenchanted, not with civilization as such, but with its excrescences; not with law, but with bad law; not with manners, but with artificial manners.

Sometimes this social criticism was eloquent and severe, sometimes it was effusively sentimental. One of its most familiar forms was praise of another culture. By extolling the virtues of the Chinese, or the Tahitians or the Americans (both red and white), the *philosophes* could expose the vices of their own society clearly enough to reach all but the most obtuse reader—and indirectly enough to escape officious censors.

Their favourite culture for this purpose was the Chinese. China was remote enough from European civilization for Europeans to speculate freely about its manners, its religion and its institutions. Besides, the Chinese civilization was truly impressive. Ever since the 17th century, missionaries had been sending back reports about the astonishing things they witnessed daily, reports so filled with admiration and detail that European intellectuals were seized with a mania for things Chinese. *Chinoiserie* appeared on furniture and porcelain and wallpaper, and French ladies twirled umbrellas copied from the Chinese parasol. Operas and plays had Chinese themes, and Chinese gardens sprang up on country estates all over Europe. But the impact of China on Western philosophy was of far greater and more lasting significance. The German philosopher Christian Wolff raised a storm at the University of Halle by implying that the wisdom of Confucius was superior to the tenets of Christianity. And in France, Voltaire became the centre of a circle that admired Chinese culture for its antiquity, Chinese government for its tolerance, and Chinese philosophy for its concern with a pure and simple morality, with no nonsense and no metaphysics.

With the Tahitians it was different. They were thought to be superior because they lived in harmony with nature. Diderot was their most extravagant advocate. In his *Supplement to Bougainville's Travels*, inspired by Louis Antoine de Bougainville's account of his voyage around the world between 1767 and 1769, he writes of an imaginary confrontation between Tahitians and French explorers. Diderot's spokesman for the Tahitians is an elderly chief who speaks with the thoughts and phrases of an experienced philosopher. He contrasts the sexual repressions of the Christian world with the open sensuality of his own country and concludes that Christian morality leads to hypocrisy and crime, while Tahitian morality favours sincerity and happiness. This South Sea idyll was not simply a primitivist's dream. Diderot's Tahitians are rational, civilized men; they do not give in to every prompting of nature, but study what is best in it, then try to follow it honestly.

As for the Americans, red and white, they kept the social critics of the Enlightenment busy in various ways. To some, the American Indian was a "good savage"—tall, tough, simple and moral. To others, he was a degenerate and a good argument for the desirability of civilization. Similarly, the colonists were sometimes idealized as the occupants of a new Eden, and sometimes pictured as the dross of Europe living in an overseas penal colony. One group of colonists, however, was universally praised. Voltaire spoke appreciatively of William Penn and his Quakers even though he had never been to America, and visitors to Pennsylvania added their own glowing tributes. Simple and honest, hardy but not primitive, the Quakers seemed to Europeans to have all the advantages of civilization and none of the disadvantages. Benjamin Franklin reinforced this impression when he visited Paris in 1767 and 1769. Shrewdly exploiting his own personality to gain support for the American colonists, Franklin was sincere but well mannered, intelligent but unpretentious. To the *philosophes* of the Paris salons the very simplicity of his appearance seemed a powerful criticism of their own sophisticated society.

In this climate of self-criticism Jean Jacques Rousseau worked out his ideas for a better society —ideas that were widely misunderstood in his own time and continue to be so today. This was partly Rousseau's own fault. Morbid and suspicious, he turned against all his friends and turned his friends against him. It was also partly the fault of his prose, which is lively and epigrammatic in style, and invites quotation out of context. Thus he got the reputation for being a Utopian dreamer who wanted to do away with organized society and go "back to nature" and the state of the "noble savage". In fact, these were phrases that Rousseau never used, and never could have used. Rousseau said repeatedly that once man has entered society, he can never leave it; human nature does not, and should not, revert to the jungle. He said it most eloquently in his book *The Social Contract*.

When men leave the state of nature, he wrote, they undergo a remarkable change: "justice" replaces "instinct", the amoral person acquires a sense of morality. In doing so, man "deprives himself of some advantages which nature had given him", but, in return, "he acquires others so great" that were it not for the vices of society he would bless for ever the day he entered it. On that day he

"NOBLE SAVAGES", *one of the great clichés of the age, were pictured in a French account of 1777 that told how the Spaniards ravaged the Incas of Peru. Many who championed the virtues of primitive life against the corruptions of civilization attributed the phrase to Rousseau, but actually Dryden was its author.*

turns from a "stupid and unimaginative animal" into "an intelligent being, a man".

Rousseau wanted to create a civilization worthy of man, and men worthy of that civilization. Little in his early career suggested so lofty a later preoccupation. Born in Geneva in 1712 to a shiftless watchmaker, he lost his mother when he was a few days old, and was brought up by a variety of relatives and friends. At the age of 16 he set out on his own, wandering first to Italy, then to France. Along the way, he was briefly converted to Roman Catholicism and had a long, odd love affair with a Madame de Warens, who was 12 years his senior and whom he called, significantly, *Maman*. He thought for a while of becoming a priest, but gave it up; then he tried music and teaching, but lost interest in them as professions, too. His studies, however, brought him in contact with the main ideas of the Enlightenment, and when he reached Paris in the 1740's he became friendly with the leading French *philosophes*, especially Diderot.

In 1750, Rousseau gained sudden fame by winning a prize offered by the Academy of Dijon for an essay on the question of whether the arts and sciences had improved men's morals. Rousseau's answer was a ringing No: man, good and innocent by nature, had been corrupted by science, learning and the social graces.

The *Discourse on the Arts and Sciences* was a foretaste of Rousseau's subsequent concern with the problem of regenerating man and society. In 1754 a second discourse, the *Discourse on the Origins of Inequality*, describes the invention of the idea of private property as a fateful moment in human history. In this work Rousseau looks back with a certain nostalgia to a simpler state of social existence, when men were relatively equal and the bonds of affection between them were strong. But he knew, if only dimly, that there was no way of returning to this state, and much of his later, great work is devoted to exploring ways of rising to a higher one. His two undoubted masterpieces on this subject are *Emile* and *The Social Contract*. Both were published in the same year, 1762, and they should be read together. *Emile* is a treatise on a Utopian education, *The Social Contract* is a treatise on a Utopian society.

Emile, the young student in the first book, is entrusted to a tutor who reverses the usual sequence of education. Reason, which is usually one of the first of the faculties to be cultivated, in Emile is the last—because, says Rousseau, reason is the last faculty to awaken. A child develops as civilization develops—from animal to savage to reasoning human to fully formed social being—and his education should equip him for each of these stages, step by step. It is nonsense to use rote learning and rationalist arguments with children, since the first they forget, and the second they cannot grasp. A child's passions must be formed first; he must learn from actual experience, walk through fields and hills before he sees a map. Only later, when he understands what he sees, should he be taught to read—and his first book should be *Robinson Crusoe*, the epic of the life close to nature. By the time he reaches manhood, passionately involved with life, affectionate and unaffected, Rousseau's ideal young man will also know his Greek and Roman classics—and know them well.

*The Social Contract* analyses a society that could only be run successfully by a civilization of Emiles. In this book, Rousseau wrestles with the age-old political question of how to reconcile liberty and authority. Cutting through the compromises of the liberal *philosophes*, Rousseau says that man can legitimately obey orders only if he gives them himself. The good society is one in which the individual is at once ruler and subject, in which the individual makes the laws he obeys. It is a society which can function only in a small State, and only in a State whose people have a sense of responsibility. Hence Rousseau makes a famous distinction between two kinds of public opinion. In one, the "general will", a citizen recognizes the community's welfare as identical with his own, and he always supports what is right for the community. In the other, which Rousseau calls the "will of all", public opinion is simply the compilation of selfish, private points of view.

*The Social Contract* is a complicated and sometimes disquieting book. It suggests that a good society needs a kind of social religion, a creed to which all must subscribe or suffer banishment. It also suggests that the "general will" may actually be the expression of a minority—perhaps even a minority of one. Such notions have seemed suspect to later critics, especially those who have experienced the terrors of dictatorship or the manipulation of public opinion by those in authority. But this criticism misses the heart of Rousseau's ideas —the concept of individual worth.

Rousseau's cult of the individual comes through most clearly in his famous autobiography, the *Confessions*, and his equally famous novel, *La Nouvelle Héloïse*. The *Confessions* shows a fascinating if rather morbid concern with one individual, Rousseau himself. *La Nouvelle Héloïse* is the love story of two individuals, the aristocratic Julie and her commoner tutor, Saint-Preux. It is a tale of the fate of private affections when they run counter to the pressures of society. Indeed, Rousseau's exploration of the inner world of the individual, as well as his proposals for reorganizing society, mark him as a man of his age. For the 18th century was not only an age of reason, but also of sentiment. Men and women might be conscious of their obligation to the "social contract", but they were also conscious of themselves and their feelings, and they revelled in sighs and tears—and *La Nouvelle Héloïse* offered plenty of both.

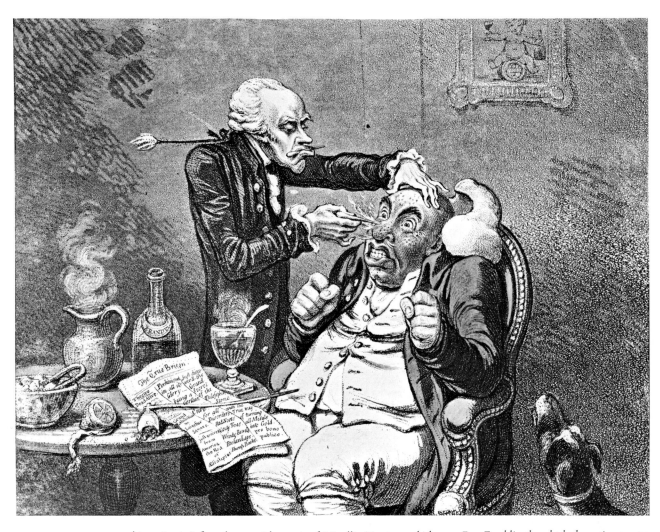

A MEDICAL QUACK *treats his patient's inflamed nose with a pair of Metallic Tractors, which even Ben Franklin thought had curative powers.*

# THE CREDULOUS ERA

In the Enlightenment's mood of optimism, the difference between open-minded-ness and gullibility was often indiscernible. The *philosophes'* insistence that old concepts be re-examined opened the door to a flock of irrational schemes and fakeries. If man's intelligence could solve all problems, then it seemed reason-able to believe that people with special gifts could manage special feats, such as discovering an alloy that could draw disease from the body (*above*). Eighteenth-century Europe became a paradise for visionaries, pseudo-scientists and outright quacks. They persuaded the educated and ignorant alike that they could per-form a variety of wonders—e.g., transmitting invisible healing powers to others, giving birth to rabbits and even corresponding with the man in the moon.

A MESMERIST *puts a woman into a trance as his assistant holds a candle that helps to fix the patient's attention. The mesmerist's hand movements are also part of the technique, which stayed popular in England and Germany after the craze died in Paris.*

# A CRAZE FOR EASY CURES

The 18th century's mania for magnetism opened a fertile field for imaginative medical men. In London Dr. James Graham built a salon where, on a Celestial Bed supported by 40 "magnetized" pillars, the impotent came to restore their powers while sniffing incense and watching erotic dances.

More lasting was the work of Franz Mesmer, who claimed to possess a healing power he called "animal magnetism". Parisians flocked to his salon to be treated by this mysterious force, which sometimes sent patients into trances—and often cured them. Most scientists mocked Mesmer, but his influence persisted; the word mesmerism still applies to his method—a form of hypnotic psychotherapy.

"ANIMAL MAGNETISM" is absorbed by fashionable Parisians from a "baquet", a big tub containing bottles of water charged with Mesmer's magical substance. Ropes transmitted the healing power to the patients' afflicted parts.

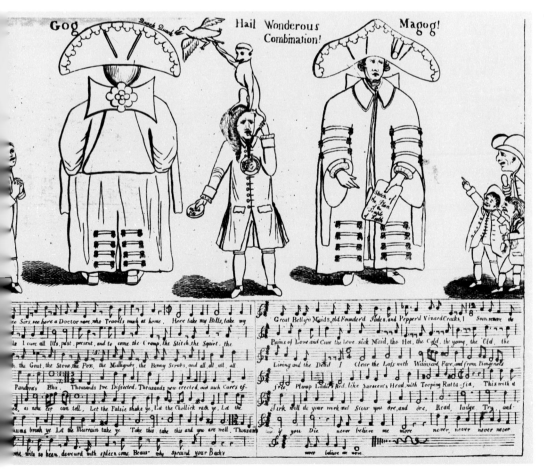

MEDICAL MONKEYSHINES are attacked in this English cartoon mocking Dr. James Graham. Gog and Magog, flanking Graham, represent the two huge door-keepers at the doctor's salon. The song lampoons Graham's treatment.

PHYSIOGNOMIST *Johann Lavater works on his theory in his study in Zürich. Lavater was a preacher and theological writer who corresponded with many philosophers, including Immanuel Kant.*

A KINGLY CHARACTER *was revealed, according to Lavater, in the eagle's eye, whose "lightning glance . . . defies the rays of the sun".*

# A GENIUS FOR MIXING SENSE WITH NONSENSE

Some of the Enlightenment's intellectual folly was conceived by well-meaning savants who worked in the fringe area between science and fantasy. The German doctor Samuel Hahnemann, for example, discovered some valuable therapeutic drugs—but he and his followers also believed in such remedies as a maiden's tear-drops and crushed bugs.

Another misguided visionary was Johann Lavater, whose science of physiognomy, illustrated here, was based on a theory that the outward appearance of all living things reflected their character. He swore he could spot a murderer by studying his face, and advised judges to dispense with normal jurisprudence, since all they had to do was follow certain physiognomic rules to tell whether an accused man was capable of committing the crime in question.

DULLNESS *was betrayed by the camel's jaw, said Lavater, who saw "no traces of courage or daring . . . between the eyes and nose".*

STUPIDITY, *of which the physiognomist noted there are several degrees, was said to show clearly in this man's strained grimace.*

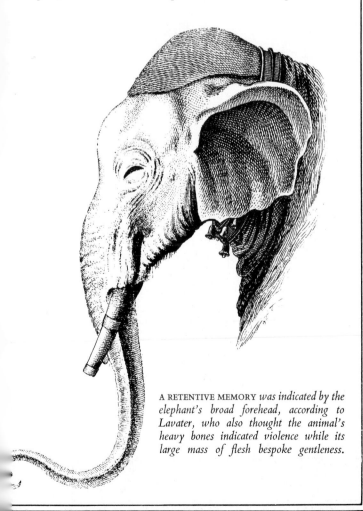

A RETENTIVE MEMORY *was indicated by the elephant's broad forehead, according to Lavater, who also thought the animal's heavy bones indicated violence while its large mass of flesh bespoke gentleness.*

A SILHOUETTE OF GOETHE, *who admired Lavater's scientific work, illustrates the use Lavater made of such images to determine the exact proportions of a man's profile and posture.*

FOOLING THE PHYSICIANS, *Mary Tofts in a Hogarth engraving "gives birth" to rabbits and rabbit parts as a midwife assists her. Mary's bizarre trick almost earned her a pension from George II after she had deceived the royal physician.*

ASSAILED BY INSULTS *from fellow Free-masons in Paris, the charlatan Cagliostro (left of table) replies in Italian: "By God, I've been found out!" Though many thought him a knave, Cagliostro had a reputation as a mighty sorcerer.*

# A BOOMING MARKET FOR FRAUDS

So gullible were the rich and fashionable of the Enlightenment that a shrewd trickster needed only audacity to leap to wealth and fame. A rude Sicilian peasant named Cagliostro became the toast of Paris when it was rumoured that he could turn pebbles into diamonds and crones into lovely maidens. The master gambler Casanova, a Venetian actor's son, built fleeting fortune and lasting fame by catering to the desires of young ladies and the superstitions of old ones. Even more outlandish was Mary Tofts, who had half of England believing she could give birth to rabbits—until she was caught bribing a servant to buy the animals at a market.

THE ACE OF HEARTS *in this caricature of Casanova symbolizes his considerable talents as a cardsharp, confidence man and lover. He also dabbled in sorcery, and convinced one patroness that he had written a letter—and received a reply—from the man in the moon.*

CRUDE FORGERIES *such as the portrait sketch above and the document below were by William Ireland. The document, with Shakespeare's arms reversed, links Ireland's ancestors with the great poet.*

A BOGUS PORTRAIT *of Shakespeare in actor's garb, fabricated by William Ireland in 1795, was widely accepted as genuine. The forger retouched an old print, adding the bard's coat of arms and listing a few plays.*

# CLUMSY DECEPTIONS
# FOR WILLING DUPES

Though 18th-century scholars prided themselves on being sceptical, many were remarkably easy to fool. In Germany, for instance, one noted professor of Natural Philosophy at the University of Würzburg was fooled into accepting as genuine crude "fossils" fabricated by his students. British scholars proved to be just as susceptible to literary hoaxes. In 1794 an 18-year-old bookseller's son, William Ireland, claimed to have uncovered scores of original Shakespeare manuscripts, including an unpublished drama entitled *Vortigern and Rowena*. For almost two years he fooled the experts; only after a noisy literary controversy and a disastrous performance of *Vortigern* was the deception unmasked. Young Ireland thereupon made a tidy profit selling forgeries of his forgeries.

FALSE FOSSILS *bearing such unlikely imprints as Hebrew inscriptions and spider webs were discovered by Professor Johann Beringer after his students had planted them in his favourite digging spots. Only when he discovered a fossil with his own name on it did the hoax became apparent to Beringer.*

THE MISSISSIPPI BUBBLE *was satirized by this Dutch cartoon of 1720. John Law, a Scottish financier who promoted the scheme in Paris, is drawn off to the poor-house by cockatrices —roosters with serpentine tails, symbols of evil. The figure in the tower warns of disaster, while in the foreground a crippled courier brings news of Britain's financial panic over the failure of the South Sea Company.*

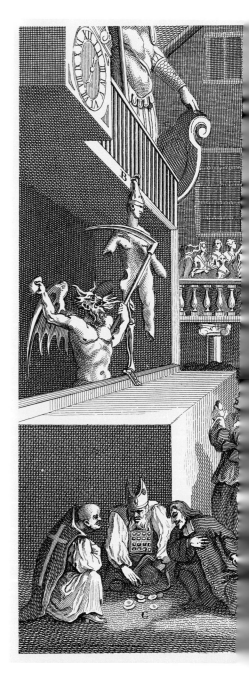

A CURIOUS ROLE *in the drama of the Mississippi bubble was played by a Parisian beggar named Bombario. He made a small fortune by circulating on the street near the stock market and leasing his humpback to stock traders as a desk on which to write orders.*

THE SOUTH SEA BUBBLE *fiasco drew the scorn of artist William Hogarth in this complex allegory. Presiding over the chaotic scene is the devil, on the left. He cuts flesh from Fortune's mutilated form and tosses titbits to his greedy worshipers (one of whom is having his pocket picked). In the shadow of Satan's shop, Churchmen, abandoning their flocks, pass the hours gambling, while Honesty, chained to a wheel, and Honour, lashed to a post, are beaten by Self-Interest and Villainy.*

# A PUBLIC BAMBOOZLED BY BUBBLES

In the Enlightenment's sanguine climate the appeal of speculation as a sure way to a fortune was irresistible. Naïve investors, confusing paper certificates with real wealth, were so eager to buy stock that at one point shares were even sold in England "for an undertaking of Great Advantage but no one to know what it is". Two ventures in particular caught the public fancy. London's South Sea Company was set up to trade with Spanish America, and Paris's Mississippi Company was founded to exploit the wealth of Louisiana. Both companies were backed by their governments, which saw the stock issues as a way to erase the public debt. Investors stampeded to speculate in what was soon worthless stock. Prices rose astronomically. In 1720 both bubbles burst. Prices plummeted, thousands were wiped out and the two governments were shaken. France was hardest hit. Its fragile economy almost collapsed and the Regent, compromised by the scheme, was forced to give up control of the government.

# 4

# A VOGUE FOR SENTIMENTALITY

When Jean Jacques Rousseau published his novel *La Nouvelle Héloïse* in 1761, thousands read it and wept, and sent Rousseau ecstatic letters to tell him so. The book was reprinted over and over again to satisfy an insatiable public. Yet there was nothing very new about *La Nouvelle Héloïse* in either plot or style. The novel was a success not because of its literary merit, but because it expressed to perfection feelings that had been springing up in western Europe in the new climate of reason—feelings for the simple virtues, for nature, for elementary conflicts between sobriety and duty and passion and pleasure.

*La Nouvelle Héloïse* was written in the form of letters, a style customary in novels of that period, and its story was the familiar one of the young girl who falls in love with her tutor. After a passionate affair the lovers part; Saint-Preux, the tutor, goes off to varied adventures; Julie, the girl, marries her father's old friend, Baron de Wolmar. She finds a degree of happiness with this disillusioned but decent man, and a certain amount of fulfilment in her two sons. But she is haunted by the memory of her premarital lapse and finally confesses to her husband, who, it turns out, has always known of the affair. Now, to wipe out the memory of the old love, Wolmar asks Saint-Preux to his country estate to tutor the boys. Saint-Preux, excitable and irresponsible, attempts to stir up the old passion; Julie, sententious and moralistic, repulses him. A little later she saves one of her sons from drowning, contracts pneumonia and dies, surrounded by adoring husband, sons and lover.

Today "sentimental" is a word of disparagement, suggesting extreme emotion lavished on trivial matters, or plain bad taste. But in the 18th century sentimentality was part of a larger process, the process by which civilization was being made more human and more humane. Then, as now, the goal was never completely attained, but the effects of the attempts to reach it were visible everywhere, in men's changing attitudes towards each other.

The first and most obvious of these was the decline of religious fanaticism. The Huguenots who had survived Louis XIV's terrible persecutions in 17th-century France found themselves not only tolerated but even permitted to practise clandes-

AN IDYLL OF FAMILY LIFE *is portrayed in this German print by the engraver Daniel Chodowiecki. Many sentimental drawings of the day attempted to make home and hearth more appealing than the glittering courts of kings.*

# The *Gentleman's Magazine:*

## St JOHN's GATE.

Lond Gazette
Lond Journ
Fog's Journ.
Applebee's ::
Read'd ; : : :
Craftsman : :
D. Spectator
Grubstreet J
Wkly Register
Free-Briton.
Hyp; Doctor
Daily Courat
Daily Post
Dai. Journal
Dai. Post-boy
D. Advertiser
Evening Post
St James's Eb.
Whitehall Eb
Lond. Eb Eg
Flying Post

Work News
Dublin 5 ::
Edinburgh 2
Briſtol ::: ::
Norwich 2
Exeter 2 : : :
Worcester
Northamton
Gloucester : :
Stamford : :
Nottingham
Bury Journ.
Chester ditto
Derby ditto
Ipswich do.
Reading do.
Leeds Merc.
Newcastle C.
Canterbury
Durham
Kendal
Boston : : ¶
Barbados;
Jamaica &c

## For JANUARY, 1731.

### CONTAINING,

/more in Quantity, and greater Variety, than any Book of the kind and Price/.

I. A View of the Weekly *Eſ-ſays* and *Controverſies,* viz. Of Q. *Elizabeth*; Miniſters; Treaties; Liberty of the Preſs; Riot Act; Armies; Traytors; Patriots; Reaſon; Criticiſm; Verſifying; Ridicule; Humours; Love; Pro-ſtitutes; Muſick; Pawn-Brokers; Surgery; Law.

II. POETRY, *viz.* The *Ode* for the New Year, by *Colly Cibber,* Eſq; Remarks upon it; Imitations of it, by way of *Burleſque;* Ver-ſes on the ſame Subject; ingenious Epitaphs and Epigrams.

III. *Domeſtick* Occurrences, *viz.*

Births, Deaths, Marriages, Pre-ferments, Caſualties, Burials and Chriſtenings in *London.*

IV. Melancholy Effects of Creduli-ty in *Witchcraft.*

V. Prices of Goods and Stocks, and a Liſt of Bankrupts.

VI. A correct Liſt of the Sheriffs for the current Year.

VII. Remarkable *Advertiſements.*

VIII. *Foreign* Affairs, with an Intro-duction to this Year's Hiſtory.

IX. Books and Pamphlets publiſh'd.

X. Obſervations on *Gardening,* and a Liſt of Fairs for the Seaſon. With a *Table* of *Contents.*

### The FIFTH EDITION.

#### By *SYLVANUS URBAN,* Gent.

*LONDON:* Printed by E. CAVE at St JOHN's GATE, and Sold by the Bookſellers of Town and Country.

EARLY PERIODICALS *had something for everyone: subject matter ranged from politics to witchcraft. In the publication above, Samuel Johnson sometimes reported Parliamentary debates (which was forbidden) as "speeches in the Great Senate of Lilliput".*

tinely some of the professions denied them by law. In England, Roman Catholics and Protestant Dissenters still suffered annoying civil disabilities (they were not allowed to attend a university or hold public office), but they were otherwise able to lead peaceful, prosperous lives. And in Prussia refugees from religious persecution in other countries were made welcome by rulers like Frederick William I and his more famous son, Frederick the Great, who declared that "in this country every man must go to heaven his own way".

There were also articulate champions for another minority, children. Rousseau in his treatise on the ideal education of a young man, *Emile,* urged that the young be given perfect freedom to develop naturally. Children became more precious. Benevolent citizens donated money to foundling hospitals; educators inveighed against ignorant and callous teachers; moralists preached the virtues of family life. It was a distinct difference from the attitudes of two centuries before, when the French essayist Montaigne, who was not a cruel man by 16th-century standards, could remark quite coolly that he had "lost two or three children in their infancy, not without regret, but without great sorrow".

The French social critic Abbé de Saint-Pierre gave this new spirit the name *bienfaisance,* and the English novelist Henry Fielding called it "goodness of heart". Even accused criminals benefited from it. In Britain, where petty crimes against property were subject to the death penalty, juries often refused to convict. In France, where Voltaire exposed the cruelty of criminal trials and gave them international notoriety, torture and mutilation became rare. At last the process of justice was coming to deserve its name.

Goodness of heart did not, however, govern all human relations. As industrialism spread in the second half of the 18th century, its victimized workers included children who dragged buckets of coal in the mines and worked as long as 15 hours a day in the textile shops—and were sometimes kept in irons at the machines they tended. Yet even in the mines and workshops the seeds of decency were being planted. In his famous *Wealth of Nations*, first published in 1776 and rapidly exalted into the bible of the new industrial order, Adam Smith declared that the prosperity of society depended on the prosperity of its workers. Smith's own sympathies obviously lay far more with the labourers than with their masters. And the French essayist Charles Duclos spoke at mid-century of "the victims of toil" and found widespread support.

"Certainly there are still barbarians", Diderot has one of his characters say in his play *Le Fils Naturel*; "when won't there be? But the time of barbarism is past. The century has become enlightened. Reason has grown more refined and the nation's books are filled with its precepts. The books that inspire benevolence in men are practically the only ones read." This was the spiritual climate in which men and women wept through 72 editions of Rousseau's *La Nouvelle Héloïse*.

Seventy-two editions imply a reading public of considerable size, and although there are few statistics, the implication is probably true. Especially in Protestant countries, where the Church was eager to get the Bible into as many hands as possible, reading had become a widespread habit by the 17th century. By the 18th century it was even more firmly entrenched. In 1781 Samuel Johnson, author of the first great dictionary of the English language, called the English "a nation of readers". Doubtless he exaggerated, but there was a general impression, shared by Englishmen and foreign visitors alike, that a great many Englishmen were literate and did indeed read a great deal. The price of books was high, but for those who could not afford to acquire their own, there were circulating libraries. And in France, where, a century before, Molière had made

fun of the bourgeois yearning for culture in his play *Le Bourgeois Gentilhomme*, that passion for culture had raised the literacy rate in the 18th century to approximately 7 out of every 10 French adults.

This growing literacy exacted its price. The new readers came, naturally enough, from increasingly lower levels of education and taste. Many of them were ready only for trash—for the sensational political gossip of certain periodicals and for highly coloured tales of the lives of notorious criminals. Even the best of writers made compromises with this public. The high style once favoured by the literary set faded—a style associated in France with the neo-classical tragedies of Corneille and Racine, and in England with the elegant comedies of Wycherley and Congreve. But writers also took it upon themselves to raise the level of the new reading public. Novels and periodicals became deliberately and successfully educational and concerned with moral issues.

Among the many periodicals that sprang up to serve this purpose were Daniel Defoe's *Review*, first published in 1704, and *The Tatler* of Joseph Addison and Richard Steele, first published in 1709. But the most famous of the enlightening journals, despite its short life, was *The Spectator*, written largely by Addison, with the active help of Steele and an occasional contribution from such men as Jonathan Swift. *The Spectator* appeared daily, except Sunday, from the 1st March 1711, to the 6th December 1712, and was briefly revived in 1714. Its purpose, Addison told his readers, was "to make their instruction agreeable, and their diversion useful. For which reasons I shall endeavour to enliven morality with wit, and to temper wit with morality". Just as Socrates had "brought Philosophy down from heaven, to inhabit among men", so Addison similarly proposed to bring "Philosophy out of closets and libraries, schools and colleges, to dwell in clubs and assemblies, at tea-tables and in coffee-houses".

*The Spectator's* articles are entries in the fictitious journal of a Mr. Spectator. They record the adventures, conversations and reflections of the members of a small and congenial club whose personalities are a cross-section of the British middle classes. There is a clergyman, "a very philosophic man, of general learning, great sanctity of life, and the most exact good breeding", and a bachelor attorney, "a member of the Inner Temple". There is also a military man, "a gentleman of great courage, good understanding, but invincible modesty", and a well-bred but susceptible man-about-town, Will Honeycomb, on whom, "having been very careful of his person, and always had a very easy fortune, time has made but very little impression, either by wrinkles on his forehead, or traces on his brain". A fifth member is Sir Andrew Freeport, a merchant "of indefatigable industry, strong reason, and great experience". And finally, there is Sir Roger de Coverley, a lovable, eccentric country squire who rapidly became the club's leading character.

Sir Roger and his friends, addressing themselves to a non-philosophical audience, taught philosophy by example. Their ideas of virtue and goodness of heart were embedded in essays that made fun of crudeness at table, praised decency of language and restraint in wit, ridiculed affection and pomposity, and preached family affection and kindness to women and children. Occasionally there was a straightforward literary essay in praise of the poetry of Milton, or the sentiments in certain popular ballads, or the pleasures of the imagination—"for by this Faculty a Man in a Dungeon is capable of entertaining himself with Scenes and Landskips more beautiful than any that can be found in the whole Compass of Nature".

Meanwhile the great poets and prose writers of the age—Swift and Alexander Pope, and their friends —continued to address the old *élite* in rather differ-

ent tones, but with similar ends in mind. A great civilization, still traditional in its outward forms but modern in its energies, was growing before their eyes, and the situation was at once exhilarating and bewildering. The new men of politics and commerce held out new promises, but their aggressiveness also threatened old values. One weapon against them was satire. Jonathan Swift, the most corrosive satirist of his day, used his pen to ridicule pedants in *The Battle of the Books* and theologians in *A Tale of a Tub*, but in his imperishable classic, *Gulliver's Travels*, he went after bigger game: mankind itself. No one is quite sure what Swift's private purpose was in writing *Gulliver*, but this much is clear: he was portraying man, capable of reason, failing to use reason in the one area where he needed it most, morality, and misusing it in the one area where he claimed to use it best, science.

Swift's friend, the poet Alexander Pope, was also critical of his age. Beneath the glittering surface of his elegantly rhymed couplets there are hidden depths—his poetry carries considerable critical and philosophical weight. Like the classical poets who furnished him with models, he thought it was the poet's role to instruct as well as please. In his *Essay on Criticism*, modelled on Horace's *Ars Poetica*, he laid down rules for literary artists which bade them be mindful of form; in his *Essay on Man* he lectured men on their place in the scheme of things:

> *Know then thyself, presume not God to scan;*
> *The proper study of Mankind is Man.*

But Pope's moralizing had puzzling overtones. Although he was, and remained, a Roman Catholic, he echoed the deists' fervent belief in an unvarying regulated universe—a concept incompatible with the Christian belief in miracles. And while the main targets of his satire were serious and richly deserving of scorn, he often used his pen to settle personal scores. In the *Dunciad* he not only attacks dullness, pettiness and mediocrity, but also stoops to pay off literary adversaries.

For all the intensity of his anger, Pope was too formal, too classical in style to suit popular tastes. The admiration of the wider reading public was reserved for a new literary form, the novel. In England, this public read the works of Samuel Richardson, Henry Fielding and Laurence Sterne; in France it read Abbé Prévost; in Germany, Goethe. And all over Europe it read Rousseau. The 18th-century novel was the descendant of an earlier, unbuttoned kind of literature, the romance and the picaresque tale. Like them, it was permissive in style—composed of informal meanderings and asides, and often written as a series of letters. The novelist could dwell on sentiments that poets writing in the decorous style of classical tradition could only hint at.

In 1752 Lady Mary Wortley Montagu, a bluestocking brought up as a good classicist, nevertheless wrote to her daughter about Richardson's *Clarissa:* "I was such an old fool as to weep over Clarissa Harlowe, like any milkmaid of sixteen over the ballad of the Lady's Fall. To say truth, the first volume softened me by a near resemblance of my maiden days; but on the whole 'tis most miserable stuff. . . . [Clarissa] follows the maxim . . . of declaring all she thinks to all the people she sees, without reflecting that in this mortal state of imperfection, fig leaves are as necessary for our minds as our bodies, and 'tis as indecent to show all we think as all we have".

Despite Lady Mary's reservations, the sentimental novelists—and later the sentimental playwrights —were breaking down the distinctions between what was public and what was private, to show all that men thought and felt. Clearly, such breaches of decorum appealed more to the new public than the old. It was the middle orders of society—men and women well-off but not socially distinguished, edu-

cated but not learned—who bought the novels and wept over them so copiously. In Richardson's own time Lord Chesterfield disdainfully observed of *Clarissa* that "the middle classes for whom it was written, and whose tone and sentiment it may be taken to justly represent, were seized with wild enthusiasm for it". Lord Chesterfield, who claimed that *Clarissa* bored him, may have started the fashion for calling the novel a bourgeois art form. But this handy theory excludes some important exceptions. Many aristocrats read and enjoyed novels, too. And while novelists did indeed address themselves primarily to a middle-class audience, they did so in widely different ways.

Samuel Richardson, for example, was interested in the secrets of psychology—although he did not, of course, give it that name. A printer by trade, Richardson was compiling a volume of model letters for "country readers who were unable to indite for themselves". Among his models were some he hoped would "instruct handsome girls, who were obliged to go out to service, as we phrase it, how to avoid the snares that might be laid against their virtue". From this occupation grew his first novel, *Pamela, or Virtue Rewarded*, published in 1740, which portrays the adventures of a virtuous servant girl whom her amorous master first tries to seduce and ends by marrying. It was an immediate and popular success.

*Clarissa, or the History of a Young Lady* followed it and might very well have been subtitled "Virtue Punished". Endlessly and in exhaustive detail, it recounts the adventures of a young lady who resists the brutal importunities of her self-righteous and narrow-minded family to marry a suitor whom she detests. In her misery, Clarissa turns to Lovelace, a young rake, appealing but irresponsible and violent. She leaves home, resists Lovelace's attempts to seduce her, and, throughout a series of sordid episodes in which her ruthless lover drugs and

rapes her, retains her lofty morals. When Lovelace, the conqueror conquered, asks to marry her, she refuses and dies of shame.

Merely to recite this melodramatic plot is to do Richardson an injustice. His tale, for all its bathos, is full of psychological insights into human emotions and unpleasant, often pathological behaviour. "If you were to read Richardson for the story," observed the shrewd Samuel Johnson, foremost literary critic of the day, "your impatience would be so much fretted that you would hang yourself. But you must read him for the sentiment."

Richardson's success was legendary, not only in England but also on the Continent. Diderot said he would put Richardson on the same shelf with Moses, Homer, Sophocles and Euripides. But in the chorus of praise there were a few dissenters. Among them was Henry Fielding, a gentleman by birth, a playwright and novelist by vocation, and in his later life

a fine, humane judge at Westminster, where he practised the goodness of heart he preached in his writings. Fielding despised Richardson's novels for their heavy-handed moralizing, and made fun of his *Pamela* in a burlesque, *An Apology for the Life of Mrs. Shamela Andrews*. A year later, with the publication of *Joseph Andrews*, he began writing on his own, and in 1749 he produced *The History of Tom Jones, a Foundling*.

*Tom Jones* is a big novel, filled with life. Its characters, some good, others evil, are not caricatures but real people, driven by their passions and their need for love, or by inner urges they do not understand. Fielding tells their stories and philosophizes over them with amused tolerance and genial wisdom; he finds even sinners acceptable.

Yet Fielding does not gloss over reality. Life in 18th-century England was harsh, and Fielding's portrait of the English scene has as many shadows as it has lights. Reality, he says, is neither wholly bland nor wholly seamy; it is both, and it is the task of the novelist to capture both. In his "bill of fare" in the opening chapter of *Tom Jones*, he announces that his subject is "Human Nature", which is of "such prodigious variety, that a cook will have sooner gone through all the several species of animal and vegetable food in the world, than an author will be able to exhaust so extensive a subject".

Fielding captured human nature through external action—through incident and the clash of character. Laurence Sterne, writing a decade later, captured it by following the internal process of thought, a device not unlike today's stream-of-consciousness writing. He was dramatizing John Locke's theory of the association of ideas. Locke said that all ideas originated in sensory experiences, that these acted upon the mind to produce ideas, but that the order and association of the ideas was not under the mind's control; the mind was simply the passive recipient.

Sterne translated this into a kind of writing that attempted to express life as it is actually experienced and thoughts as they actually occurred. His masterpiece is *Tristram Shandy*, a voluminous, experimental novel that meanders through the mind of the hero, violates chronology, plays with language, inserts seemingly irrelevant anecdotes, and attempts to proceed much as thought was supposed to proceed: in accordance with hidden rules that appear on the surface as chaos. To support his design, Sterne deliberately confuses his reader; he leaves pages blank, mislabels chapter headings, and indulges in typographical eccentricities unmatched for daring until the 20th century.

Writers on the Continent also experimented with the novel. Although it did not become important as a form of literature in Germany until Goethe published his *Sorrows of Young Werther* in the 1770's, there were novels in France as early as in England.

## "CLARISSA":

## A LOVERS' CONFRONTATION

*Like many popular novels it inspired, "Clarissa" was melodramatic, moralizing, endlessly meandering and written as a series of letters that revealed its characters' every emotion. Below, Lovelace, a rake, tells a friend of surprising his lady at an inn.*

". . . Oh! there he is! said she, and threw her apron over her face. I cannot see him!—I cannot look upon him! Begone, begone! touch me not!

"For I took her struggling hand, beseeching her to be pacified; and assuring her that I would make all up with her upon her own terms and wishes.

"Base man! said the violent lady, I have no wishes, but never to behold you more! Why must I be thus pursued and haunted? Have you not made me miserable enough already? Despoiled of all succour and help, and of every friend, I am contented to be poor, low, and miserable, so I may be free from your persecutions. . . .

"I told you so! whisperingly said I . . . shaking my head with a face of great concern and pity; and then to my charmer, My dear creature, how you rave! . . . Have patience, my love. Be pacified, and we will coolly talk this matter over: for you expose yourself, as well as me: these ladies [in the room] will certainly think you have fallen among robbers, and that I am the chief of them.

"So you are! so you are! stamping, her face still covered (*she thought of Wednesday night, no doubt*); and sighing as if her heart were breaking, she put her hand to her forehead—I shall be quite distracted!

"I will not, my dearest love, uncover your face. You shall *not* look upon me, since I am so odious to you. But this is a violence I never thought you capable of.

"And I would have pressed her hand, as I held it, with my lips; but she drew it from me with indignation.

"Unhand me, sir, said she. I will not be touched by you. Leave me to my fate. What right, what title, have you to persecute me thus? . . ."

Abbé Prévost's famous *Manon Lescaut* appeared in 1731, even before Richardson's *Pamela*. *Manon* is the tale of the Chevalier des Grieux and his fatal infatuation with the courtesan Manon, who ruins his life and her own. She is exiled to America, he goes with her, and she dies, ennobled by love and suffering, in the first of a series of edifying 18th-century deathbed scenes. Compared to the grand passions of 17th-century tragedy, the amorous escapades of this unhappy pair are trivial. *Manon* was unquestionably a new kind of book addressed to a new kind of audience.

The same audience also found much to admire on the stage, where fashions too had changed. The contrast between 17th and 18th-century drama is enormous. The neoclassical plays of the 17th century had obeyed the time-honoured rules of unity of time, place and action. Events depicted could span no more time than the play itself, and the setting had to remain constant. Typically they were set in vast halls, and much of the action was the comings and goings of messengers reporting what was happening elsewhere, or what had happened the day or the year before.

Neoclassical drama had also assigned emotions to characters strictly according to class. Only kings and queens, noblemen and noblewomen had passions worthy of tragedy; the bourgeois and the peasantry, when they were introduced at all, were introduced as figures of fun. Even Shakespeare made princes the spokesmen for his most eloquent speeches, and ordinary men the vehicles of comic relief. But Shakespeare also defied the canons of neoclassical drama. He wove low comedy into high tragedy, and, instead of declaiming about violent events, showed them in action on stage. Too talented to be disdained and too "irregular" to be fully appreciated, he affected many neoclassical writers much as he affected Voltaire, who both admired him and called him a drunken barbarian.

Nevertheless it was partly through Shakespeare's example that a new kind of play arose. By the 18th century the cross-breeding of tragedy and comedy was widespread. Tearful comedies introduced sentiment into a form of drama that had traditionally been either purely bawdy or purely satirical—depending on whether the comedy was low or high. Similarly, bourgeois tragedies exalted the emotions of merchants to dimensions formerly reserved for royalty. The credit for the growth of these new dramatic *genres* belongs again to the British, specifically to British middle-class morality. The blatant immorality of the Restoration stage brought protests so vehement that not even the standard excuse was acceptable—that the portrayal of vice was designed to censor, not celebrate, such behaviour. Consequently, Restoration playwrights began to inject moralizing messages into their dramas. Rakes were still rakes, but their adventures brought them suffering and eventual promises to reform.

Then, in 1731, the playwright George Lillo caught this new mood to perfection in his bourgeois tragedy *The London Merchant; or, the History of George Barnwell*, and others rushed to follow him. George is an honest young apprentice who is victimized by an experienced and villainous harlot and descends melodramatically into a life of crime; he robs his master, kills his uncle, and finally repents and is executed. Today *The London Merchant* seems poor stuff, but in its own time it impressed such discriminating men of letters as Diderot and the German dramatist Gotthold Lessing. In 1755 Lessing tried his hand at a similar kind of tragedy in *Miss Sara Sampson*, and shortly thereafter Diderot published two domestic dramas, *Le Fils Naturel* and *Le Père de Famille*, both of them moralizing, sentimental affairs. The emotional conflicts of ordinary people had become as important as those of the heroes in Greek tragedy. Clearly, the age of kings was on the wane, even in the theatre.

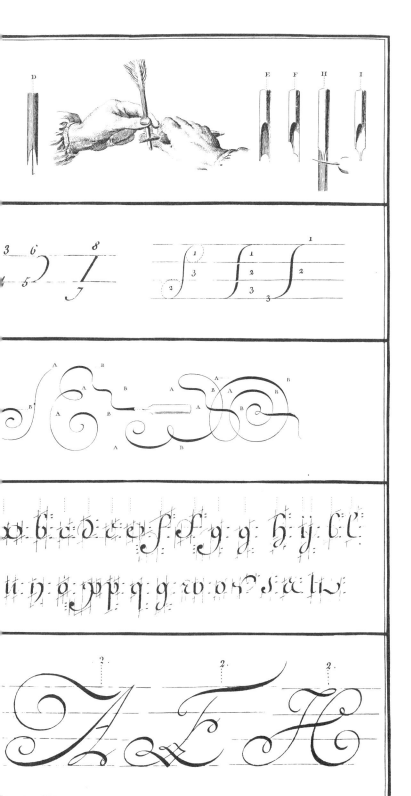

THE ART OF HANDWRITING *in the Enlightenment demanded, according to Denis Diderot's Encyclopaedia, "all the forms which spirit can furnish and hand can execute". The sketches show, from the top: (1) cutting the quill point; (2) basic lines and curves; (3) flourishes; (4) letters; (5) capitals.*

It was also on the wane in the writing of history. Harking back to the ancient Greek and Roman historians for pleasure and instruction, the *philosophes* admired such men as Thucydides and Tacitus for their suspicion of fables, their penetrating inquiry into the real motives for men's actions, and their insistence on ascribing historical events to natural causes. This sort of history had long been out of fashion. In medieval times, under the influence of Christian scholasticism, history had become a grand drama whose sole purpose was to reveal divine Providence; historical events were prophecies, to be read as clues to the end of history, the apocalypse. Renaissance historians had offered some secular alternatives to this exclusively theological view, and 17th-century historians had been concerned about method and the authenticity of documents.

But essentially the medieval approach to history changed very little until the Enlightenment, and it was against this view that the historians of the Enlightenment took their stand. Dropping all attempts to find supernatural causes for historical events, eschewing court gossip as a source of facts, devoting less space to battles and more to large cultural themes, they wrote a new kind of history. It was a history concerned with philosophy and science, with the development of such arts as the theatre, with the relation between religion and foreign policy. In short, it was social history.

One of the earliest of the 18th-century social historians was Montesquieu. His essay *Considerations on the Causes of the Greatness and Decline of the Romans* is hardly great history—in its reliance on ancient authorities it is often naïve and capricious. But it does at least break with the medieval custom of assigning supernatural causes to worldly events. Rome rose and fell not because God first cherished and then punished the Romans, but because various social, political and geographical conditions forced the Romans to establish and then destroy both the Republic of Rome and the Empire.

The first accomplished master of the new history was Voltaire, whose *History of Charles XII*, published in 1731, attempted to explain the career of the odd Swedish monarch by examining the character of the man himself. Voltaire describes Charles as half Alexander the Great, half Don Quixote. But Charles's life invited melodrama, and Voltaire's book sacrificed history for the sake of excitement. He did not really hit the mark until two later productions. In 1751 he published the *Age of Louis XIV*, a brilliant treatment of a brilliant age, filled with deft portraits, deep perceptions and solidly grounded judgements. And in 1756 he published the first version of his *Essay on the Manners and Spirit of the Nations* (it was several times revised and enlarged). The *Essay* was history treated with a universality no one had ever attempted before. Marred by anticlerical propaganda and an inadequate sympathy for the Middle Ages, its grand sweep, natural explanations for events and light-hearted erudition nevertheless set a model that many admired and tried to imitate.

In Britain, meanwhile, *philosophes* were producing excellent histories of their own. William Robertson's histories of Scotland, of Charles V and of America were remarkable for their learning and literary merit, and—even more unusual for the time—their fair-minded treatment of Christianity. David Hume wrote a voluminous *History of England*, which was popular and influential despite its generosity to the unpopular house of Stuart, especially Charles I. But the undoubted masterpiece of them all, the greatest historical work of the 18th century was Edward Gibbon's *History of the Decline and Fall of the Roman Empire*.

Gibbon, a fat, gaudily dressed man, less than five feet tall, was a convert first to Roman Catholicism and then to scepticism. Never in danger of marriage after an early engagement which his father commanded him to break, he devoted his life to literary pursuits. He served for a time in the British Army and the House of Commons, two experiences he put to use as he mused on his history of Rome. He was a superb stylist, a deft and feline ironist and a complete unbeliever.

Gibbon's panorama of Roman history opens with a majestic account of the Empire under the Antonines, happy but corrupt, its energy sapped by long peace. Then he describes the centuries of decay: invasion by Germanic tribes from the north, subversion by the spread of Christianity within the Empire. The threat of the first was obvious, but the second, wrote Gibbon, was more insidious: Christianity was fatal to the Empire because it encouraged withdrawal from life, preached asceticism and the Second Coming, and, while waiting for that peaceable event, quarrelled with everyone. Though Gibbon was too careful an historian and too subtle a man to attribute Rome's fall to these causes alone, the theme of the *Decline and Fall* is the double triumph of barbarism and religion. Contemporary Christians regarded his history as an attack on their faith, and they were right.

Indeed, great as the *philosophes*' historical writings were, and much as they advanced the profession, they suffered from this and one other defect. Anti-Christian spleen led them to turn history into a polemic argument instead of trying to understand it. And a rather elementary conception of human nature led them to assign the causes for human behaviour to bundles of mechanical impulses. Thus, the histories of the age mirrored its limitations as well as its new way of life. These limitations help to explain why the Enlightenment sometimes tended to confuse morality with science and in fact called the social sciences "moral sciences". For the men of the Enlightenment, human conduct was to be judged as well as studied; their ultimate goal was not simply good men, but good men in a good society.

AN ENGLISHMAN ABROAD, *Thomas Coke, 18, is dressed for a fancy ball in this portrait painted in Rome.*

# THE GRAND TOUR

Travel was a natural expression of the Enlightenment's interest in new vistas, and wealthy Englishmen regarded the Grand Tour—a round of Europe's cities— as indispensable to their education. Admiring almost everything French and Italian, they thought the Tour worth more than going to the university. When Thomas Coke (*above*) finished school in 1771, his great-aunt wrote, "Sir, I understand you have left Eton and probably intend to go to one of those Schools of Vice, the Universities. If, however, you choose to travel I will give you 500 pounds per annum". Coke was quick to pick the Tour. So did many others; in one peak year the Continent was crowded with about 40,000 Englishmen.

VIENNA

MUNICH

VENICE

*ADRIATIC SEA*

ROME

NAPLES

*MEDITERRANEAN SEA*

# HITTING THE HIGH SPOTS OF EUROPE

Since the Grand Tour was intended to be more edifying than amusing, a young English sojourner almost always travelled with a tutor to supervise his lessons and his conduct.

The crossing from Dover to Calais took anywhere from 3 to 12 hours and was often uncomfortably rough. In Paris the Englishman's objective was to shed his simple periwig for a powdered coiffure and to acquire sophistication. From France he went on to Italy, which posed something of a problem: if he went by ship he ran the risk of encountering pirates; if he went overland he had to go by sedan chair through Alpine passes—where, as one terrified tourist pointed out, "there was scarce room for a cloven foot".

In Italy Anglican tutors kept a wary eye on the popish lures of Rome, but the stripling was on his own against the worldly temptations of Venice and the occasional eruptions of Vesuvius. Most Grand Tourists never got farther than Italy, but a diligent few went on to German-speaking Europe. Fortitude was required because, though Vienna was eminently civilized, German inns were infested with bugs and thieves, and customs inspectors at every border were meddlesome and officious.

Finally, after from one to five years abroad, the edified traveller could return with confidence to England and demonstrate, as one poet wryly remarked, "How much a dunce, that has been sent to roam, / Excels a dunce, that has been kept at home".

# PARIS: CITY OF CONTRASTS

In Paris the typical English traveller underwent a dazzling metamorphosis. After renting rooms in the fashionable quarter of St. Germain, and hiring servants, he exchanged his sombre clothes for a silk suit trimmed with lace. He took lessons in fencing, riding and French conversation. He learned how to hold a cane and how to woo a lady with gallantries. Finally he was ready to enter high society and court life at Versailles. However, the Englishman's love for Paris was mixed with a large dose of contempt. He found its aristocrats foppish and superficial, its restaurants mediocre and its common people unpleasantly poor. In public places such as Les Halles, he was beset by beggars and pickpockets. Worst of all, the princely homes were too cold for comfort and the great ladies so heavily rouged that their countenances, in the opinion of one tourist, "seem to have no resemblance to human faces".

THE PLEASURES OF THE POOR *included dancing in the street on public holidays. The celebration shown here is taking place near the wooden sheds of Les Halles, the food market in the centre of Paris that dates back to the 12th century. On the left, an aristocratic sightseer and her children watch the sport.*

THE RESIDENCE OF ROYALTY, *12 miles outside Paris at Versailles, forms a back-cloth for rows of uniformed guards on parade. English tourists, though often overwhelmed by Versailles, stoutly maintained, along with Tobias Smollett, "that the king of England is better, I mean more comfortably, lodged".*

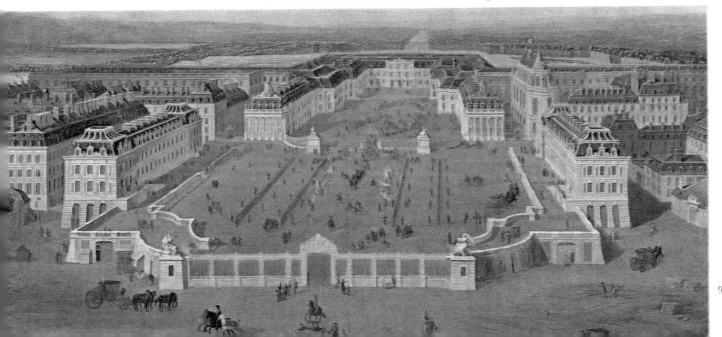

91

# A HAVEN FOR TOURING CONNOISSEURS

After the excitement of Paris, the English tourist found the slow pace of life in Florence a relief. The lazy visitor, wrote poet Thomas Gray, could "get up at twelve o'clock, breakfast till three, dine till five, sleep till six, drink cooling liquors till eight, go to the bridge till ten, sup till two, and so sleep till twelve again". The more ambitious tourist, however, studied art in the Uffizi Gallery, particularly in a room called the Tribuna, shown here, where the best paintings and Greek sculptures were housed. The English envoy to Florence, Sir Horace Mann, came here with visiting countrymen to discuss art with a museum official, Bianchi. (Bianchi was highly admired by the connoisseurs until he robbed the gallery and set it on fire.) Eventually, the Tribuna became such an English mecca that the royal family commissioned the painter Johann Zoffany to do this crowded, busy group portrait of Englishmen abroad.

GUIDE TO A GALLERY, *the key above identifies some of the men and works of art in the picture. (A) Carracci, "A Bacchante"; (B) an anonymous pupil of Raphael, "St. John the Baptist"; (C) Guido Reni, "Cleopatra"; (D) Rubens, "Portrait of Justus Lipsius and His Pupils"; (E) Raphael, "Madonna of the Chair"; (F) Correggio, "Adoration of the Child"; (G) Raphael, "Madonna of the Goldfinch"; (H) Rubens, "Allegory of War"; (I) Lord Cowper; (J) Johann Zoffany with Raphael's "Cowper Madonna"; (K), (L), (M), (N) four Greek sculptures: "Faun with a Scabellum", "The Wrestlers", "Venus de' Medici", "The Knife-Grinder"; (O) Bianchi holding a Titian, "The Venus of Urbino"; (P) Sir Horace Mann.*

DECORATED BARGES *line the Grand Canal as elegant spectators observe a race during a regatta in Venice. These aquatic festivities were widely copied on the lakes and rivers of other European cities, where they were known as "Venetian nights".*

A VENETIAN STREET SCENE *features a charlatan holding aloft a tooth he has just pulled. The patient, his mouth held open by an unkempt, bespectacled assistant, writhes in pain. Passers-by, masked for Carnival, pay little heed to the operation.*

THE GILDED INTERIOR *and high altar of St. Mark's Cathedral were considered ostentatious by Englishmen. The words "Verona Fidelis" on the banner refer to the loyal city of Verona, ruled by Venice.*

# THE MANY DELIGHTS OF VENICE

Winter was Carnival time in Venice, and during the season as many as 30,000 tourists flocked to the city of canals to take in its heady pleasures. Amid the Byzantine splendour of St. Mark's Square, the visitor mingled with cosmopolitan crowds from all over Europe and the Near East. Even the most jaded sightseer was dazzled at the masquerades, regattas, comedies, operas and the dancing in the streets.

Venice was notorious for its women, and it was clearly understood that they were one of the chief attractions for young Englishmen doing the Grand Tour. As Samuel Johnson commented: "If a young man is wild, and must run after women and bad company, it is better this should be done abroad".

AN ANTIQUARY'S SHOP *in Naples is crowded with foreign souvenir shoppers. One man by the door examines a ring while another to the right admires a cameo. Although some Englishmen on the Grand Tour acquired masterpieces, many less discerning ones were duped into buying fakes at fabulous prices.*

MOUNT VESUVIUS, *which during the 18th century erupted several times, was a prime attraction for tourists. Some went to the crater on mules or in sedan chairs; others preferred viewing it from Naples. The distance, one woman explained, "almost admits examination, and certainly excludes immediate fear".*

THE RUINS OF POMPEII *emerge as workmen haul volcanic debris in wheelbarrows during excavations sponsored partly by the English. In 1710 a well-digger discovered the ancient amphitheatre at Herculaneum, and in 1748 an Italian peasant fell down his well shaft into what turned out to be Pompeii.*

il padrone
di questo Cappello
dipinse Napoli
1795

# ON THE TRAIL OF THE CLASSICAL PAST

The two ancient Roman towns of Herculaneum and Pompeii, buried by an eruption of Mount Vesuvius in the first century A.D., were rediscovered in the 18th century, and a burning desire to see them seized almost every Grand Tourist. Pompeian styles became so popular that they sparked the neoclassical revival, and by 1790 an English writer could declare: "Every thing we now use is made in imitation of those models which have been lately discovered in Italy". Naturally, every Englishman wanted to try his hand digging at the sites. Often he was led to a spot where his guides had thoughtfully reburied a coin or a marble fragment, which he might then "discover" with the first turn of the spade.

# ROME: THE FINAL GOAL

"Rome is the great object of our pilgrimage", wrote the historian Edward Gibbon, and most Englishmen agreed. The first things travellers wanted to see were the ancient ruins, and so avid were they in collecting souvenirs that one contemporary

writer quoted Romans as saying: "Were our Amphitheatre portable, the English would carry it off".

A highlight of the visitors' exhaustive inspection of Rome —three hours a day for six weeks was the prescribed routine —was St. Peter's (*above*). At Easter time the Basilica was always crowded with tourists eager to see the pageantry. One pope, when asked to revive certain neglected Holy Week ceremonies, replied: "Why not? It will amuse the English".

# 5

# THE SCIENCE
# OF MAN

When the Scottish philosopher David Hume published his first and finest work, *A Treatise of Human Nature*, he subtitled it "An Attempt to Introduce the Experimental Method of Reasoning into Moral Subjects". The "moral subjects" to which he referred were the passions, ethics and politics of man; the "experimental method" was Newtonian science. Newton had urged men to observe, then analyse their observations, to discover the laws of the physical world. Might it not be possible, by a similar process, to discover the laws that governed the world of men and society? It was this possibility that drove the Enlightenment to study what it called the "moral sciences". Hume, in his *Treatise*, aspired to be the Newton of the "science of man".

The times were hospitable to such a project. As educated men came more and more to regard man as a superior animal or a remarkable machine, they thought it only logical to explain his behaviour in scientific terms. They also thought it logical to analyse as separate and distinct phenomena the forces that moved men and societies. The 18th century was the great century of specialization and division—of labour, and of knowledge. It was in this century that physics, astronomy, mechanics, chemistry, psychology and epistemology gradually broke away from the 17th-century's all-inclusive "natural philosophy" to become individual fields of study. Each science had its own methods and attracted its own disciples, although there were, just as there are today, some men who worked in more fields than one.

One of the first of the moral sciences to feel the impact of these new conditions was the science of psychology. Ever since ancient times scholars had speculated on the faculties of reason, passion, perception and memory. But in the 17th and 18th centuries these speculations centred on the acquisition of knowledge itself—what it was, how it happened. Descartes, Hobbes, Locke and Hume had all made contributions to the understanding of the processes of perception and thought. But it was not until David Hartley published his *Observations on Man, His Frame, His Duty, and His Expectations*, in 1749, that the modern science of psychology can be said to have been born.

Hartley was a doctor who at first intended to be

a clergyman, but changed his mind when it seemed to him that his faith, although strong, was not strong enough. Nevertheless, his scientific theories had religious overtones. The loftiest goal of human behaviour was, he said, the perception of God: ". . . the idea of God, and of the Ways by which his Goodness and Happiness are made manifest, must, at last, take place of, and absorb other Ideas, and He himself become, according to the Language of the Scriptures, All in All".

The *Observations* were aimed, Hartley said, at overcoming "the great difficulty of supposing that the Soul, an immaterial Substance, exerts and receives a physical influence upon and from the Body". The link in this connection between body and soul was, he said, vibrations. These vibrations originated in sense stimuli and were carried by the nerves to the brain, where they became thought. Each sensation provoked its own individual idea. But if groups of sensations habitually occurred at the same time, their ideas became inextricably linked in the mind. Thus, one sensation could trigger a whole group of ideas and produce complex thoughts. "Any Sensations A, B, C, etc.," to quote the *Observations*, "by being associated with one another a sufficient Number of Times, get such a Power over the corresponding Ideas, a, b, c, etc., that any one of the Sensations A, when impressed alone, shall be able to excite in the Mind b, c, etc., the Ideas of the rest."

Hartley was using a mechanical principle to explain all human behaviour. Modern psychology has gone so far beyond him that his theories hardly seem relevant. But his principle of study is still important, as indeed it was in his own time. Man's mind, he said, was a legitimate subject for scientific inquiry. No one had said it quite so forcefully before.

Meanwhile other writers were exploring other aspects of human behaviour—specifically, the abnormal and irrational. David Hume declared that feelings and emotions played a greater part in human conduct than reason, and he held that this was as it should be—"reason is and ought to be the slave of the passions". Hume also argued that perceptions and convictions were not the product of rational inquiry, but of habit. In Germany, Georg Christoph Lichtenberg, professor at the University of Göttingen, recommended the scientific study of dreams, and in France Diderot casually anticipated Freud's theory of the Oedipus complex. If a child, Diderot wrote in *Rameau's Nephew*, "were left to himself and his native blindness, he would later combine the infant's reasoning with the passion of the man of thirty—he would cut his father's throat and sleep with his mother".

Two centuries later, in his *General Introduction to Psychoanalysis*, Freud seized upon this passage delightedly as evidence for his contention that men had always been aware of this unconscious drive. But it would be wrong to claim that the Enlightenment studied the unconscious systematically, or even that it fully appreciated the role of the irrational in human behaviour. Far from it. The *philosophes* did see that habit, childhood training and sheer wilfulness played important parts in the conditioning of the mind. And their theories, however inadequate, were the first steps in the scientific study of the mind. But for all their love of poetry, they gave little thought to the imagination.

Unlike psychology, a term first used in the 17th century, "sociology" was not coined until the 19th century. But the science that became sociology was seriously practised in the 18th century, and Montesquieu can legitimately be called its father. In his great treatise, *The Spirit of the Laws*, Montesquieu stated the laws that govern the shape of human societies: the kind and degree of a people's freedom is established by institutions; social and private behaviour is conditioned by climate; soil and religion influence politics. Montesquieu's method of study was roughly equivalent to modern "comparative" sociology—he assembled information on primitive and civilized societies, past and present, and compared their various features.

Meanwhile, other *philosophes*, too, began to look at societies sociologically. Voltaire and Hume, for instance, saw an intimate relation between politics, commerce and religion. Freedom of trade and freedom of opinion, they said, were inextricably linked with civil freedom, and religious tolerance appeared to be linked to commercial prosperity. The techniques of the 18th-century sociologists seem crude and primitive, but their spirit of inquiry was precisely the same as that which animates sociologists today. Eighteenth-century sociology, however, was not a neutral science. It was designed to discover the truth, but it was also designed to serve man—to find ways of making him happy by making him free. "Moral science", to the Enlightenment, read two ways: it meant using science for a moral purpose, and also making morality scientific.

The double nature of the moral sciences is most visible in what the 18th century called "political economy". The most celebrated economist of the day was Adam Smith, but Smith had distinguished predecessors. Long before the 18th century, statesmen and their advisers had speculated about the influence of the State upon the creation and distribution of wealth. The most pervasive of these speculations led to the practice of Mercantilism. According to the Mercantilists the world's resources—its land, labour and raw materials—were all elements in a finite system. Thus an increase in the resources of one State meant the decrease in the resources of another, and the economic policies of each State were consequently directed towards guarding and increasing its share of the whole.

Under Mercantilism, States hoarded precious metals, encouraged their growth of the popula-

## THE INVENTIVE URGE

*The industrial and agricultural revolutions of the 18th century produced a variety of new devices and processes, some trivial, others of lasting importance. They ranged from the deep-cutting plough above, invented by the agrarian reformer Jethro Tull, to the modern water closet and the recipe for mayonnaise. Some are listed below, with their creators and dates.*

| | | |
|---|---|---|
| SEED-PLANTING DRILL | Jethro Tull | 1701 |
| CHLORINE BLEACH | C. L. Berthollet | 1785 |
| FLYING SHUTTLE (WEAVING) | John Kay | 1733 |
| HARD PASTE PORCELAIN | Johann Böttger | 1708 |
| IRON SMELTING WITH COKE | Abraham Darby | 1709 |
| SHEFFIELD SILVER PLATE | Thomas Bolsover | 1742 |
| IMPROVED CANNON BORER | John Wilkinson | 1774 |
| MAYONNAISE | Duc de Richelieu | 1756 |
| STEAM PUMP | Thomas Newcomen | 1712 |
| BEET SUGAR EXTRACTION | Andreas Marggraf | 1747 |
| POWER LOOM | Edmund Cartwright | 1787 |
| MODERN WATER CLOSET | Joseph Bramah | 1778 |
| THRESHING MACHINE | Michael Menzies | 1732 |
| MILL-ROLLED IRON | Henry Cort | 1784 |
| STEAM ENGINE | James Watt | 1769 |
| IMPROVED LATHE | Henry Maudslay | 1800 |
| COTTON GIN | Eli Whitney | 1793 |
| WINNOWING MACHINE | James Sharp | 1777 |
| SPINNING JENNY | James Hargreaves | 1768 |

tions, founded new industries, tried to monopolize trade, prohibited skilled workers from emigrating to other countries, and strove for what they spoke of as "a favourable balance of trade"—a balance that favoured exports over imports, so that a country took in more money than it spent. Logically, this policy led to government supervision of the whole economic system. And logically, in the centuries when war was the chief instrument of national expansion, a closely regulated economy seemed appropriate: a State had to safeguard its war-making potential.

But in the 18th century the emphasis shifted from military expansion to peaceful expansion through trade. Bold merchants, wanting untrammelled profits, sought freedom to buy and sell as they chose. Slowly the conviction grew that open competition was essential to trade, that open markets did not threaten the national welfare, that the growth of a competitor's business did not automatically diminish one's own.

It was the *philosophes* who stated this most clearly. Merchants, David Hume observed, were "one of the most useful races of men". He also exposed the fallacy of hoarding money and of practising what he called "the jealousy of trade". "Not only as a man," he wrote, "but as a British subject, I pray for the flourishing commerce of Germany, Spain, Italy, and even France itself." To permit manufacturers to produce without government supervision, and merchants to trade without customs barriers, was to free men's energies and benefit everyone.

Hume's radical views were taken up by an increasing number of politicians and merchants. In France, the new ideal came to be called *laissez-faire*, and was championed by a group called the Physiocrats. François Quesnay, their founder, was court physician to Louis XV and Madame Pompadour's personal doctor. Quesnay and his followers (one of

whom was Pierre du Pont de Nemours, father of the man who founded the Du Pont industrial empire) placed a somewhat different emphasis on the philosophy of free competition; they believed that the foundation of a nation's wealth was not commerce and industry, but agriculture. The way to encourage agriculture was to remove trade restrictions, so that the farmer could be assured of a demand—and a good price—for his produce. They added, but only for the sake of economic logic, that manufacturers and merchants should also be free of trade restrictions.

In support of his theories, Quesnay drew up an elaborate and complex chart demonstrating the circulation and distribution of wealth through the various classes of society—based perhaps on the product of another physician, William Harvey, who a century before had similarly charted the circulation of blood through the body. In any case, the Physiocrats had inordinate faith in what Quesnay's chart disclosed. Their doctrine, much of which was mysticism masquerading as science, was mercilessly ridiculed by contemporary critics like Voltaire. But however misguided their premises, their teaching moved men in the direction of modern economic freedom.

Adam Smith fused the sober essays of Hume and the quixotic ideas of the Physiocrats into a consistent, rigorous science of economics. But it was still science imbued with morality. Smith described "political economy" as a "branch of the science of a statesman or legislature", and he said it had two objectives: "first, to provide a plentiful revenue or subsistence for the people, or more properly to enable them to provide such a revenue or subsistence for themselves; and secondly, to supply the State or Commonwealth with a revenue sufficient for the public services". Political economy, in other words, "proposes to enrich both the people and the sovereign". The whole Enlightenment's confidence in

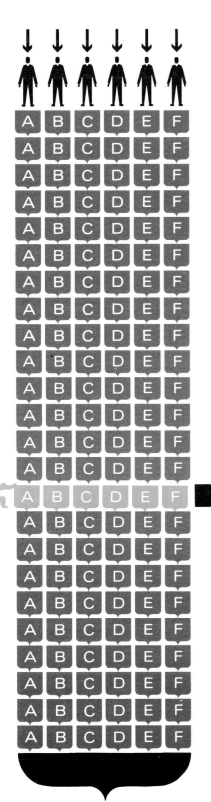

DIVISION OF LABOUR, *as developed during the Enlightenment, is symbolized in this diagram. The principle was advanced by Adam Smith in 1776. Using ordinary household pins as his example, he observed that if 10 men divided up the 18 steps necessary to make one pin, they could produce 48,000 in a day, or 4,800 per man, whereas a man working alone would be lucky to make a single one.*

**1** *Doing each step himself, one man makes one unit.*

**24**

*By specializing in one skill each, six men make 24 units in the same time.*

science's supreme ability to benefit mankind is enshrined in this definition.

*The Wealth of Nations* is Adam Smith's most famous work. But Smith himself thought of it as merely part of a larger work: the presentation of a comprehensive ethical system. *The Wealth of Nations* considered only one aspect of man: his capacity, as an economic animal, to provide himself with food and clothing and other necessary goods and services. Within this framework Smith saw self-interest as socially beneficial. If each man was free to improve his own economic position and conversely, if economic systems were free to utilize the best skills of each man, then everyone, manufacturer and labourer alike, would benefit. In Smith's optimistic view, "an invisible hand" would guide men in the pursuit of private purpose to promote simultaneously the interests of society as a whole.

But Adam Smith was not as naïve as this sounds. Although he championed free trade in principle, he conceded that there were some areas in which government restrictions might be not only useful, but even essential. He condoned, for example, the British Navigation Acts, which discouraged foreign shipping from carrying goods to and from Britain and its colonies. Obviously this was contrary to the principle of free trade, but Smith excused it on the grounds that the acts were necessary to national defence: the more merchant ships Britain had the larger its potential navy for use in time of war.

Also, he admitted that free enterprise did not automatically produce universal prosperity, since the private interests of manufacturers sometimes ran counter to the interests of the economy as a whole. He recognized, moreover, that in a free economy wages were a continuing source of conflict between masters and workers. But he advocated high wages not only as a means of making workers more productive, but as a policy beneficial for the whole society. "No society can surely be flourishing and happy," he wrote, "of which the far greater part of the members are poor and miserable. It is but equity, besides, that they who feed, cloath and lodge the whole body of the people, should have such a share of the produce of their own labour as to be themselves tolerably well fed, cloathed and lodged."

*The Wealth of Nations* opens with a famous analysis of the advantages to be gained from a division of labour. Near the end there is a moving passage which suggests some of the tragic consequences of such a division.

> *The man whose whole life is spent in performing a few simple operations, of which the effects too are, perhaps, always the same, or very nearly the same, has no occasion to exert his understanding, or to exercise his invention in finding out expedients for removing difficulties which never occur. He naturally loses, therefore, the habit of such exertion, and generally becomes as stupid and ignorant as it is possible for a human creature to become. The torpor of his mind renders him, not only incapable of relishing or bearing a part in any rational conversation, but of conceiving any generous, noble, or tender sentiment, and consequently of forming any just judgment concerning many even of the ordinary duties of private life.*

In seeing the two sides of the division of labour, Adam Smith glimpsed the potentiality for good and evil in the new industrial society that was emerging before his eyes. The Industrial Revolution was an enormously complicated series of events, some beneficial, some not. The earliest of them occurred in the 16th century, when industrial techniques became more elaborate, to be followed, in the 17th century, by the discoveries of the Scientific Revolution, which made the Industrial Revolution possible. Also, during this era the great voyages of discovery had extended trade routes

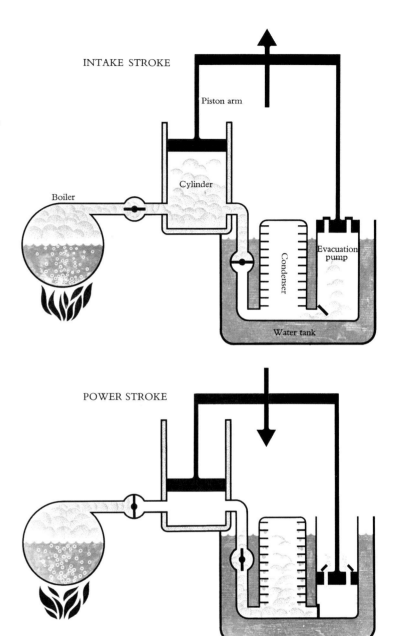

INTAKE STROKE

Piston arm

Boiler

Cylinder

Condenser

Evacuation pump

Water tank

POWER STROKE

THE FIRST EFFICIENT STEAM ENGINE *suitable for widespread industrial use was James Watt's model (diagrams above) patented in 1769. Like earlier steam engines, it used the vacuum created by condensing low-pressure steam (the expansive power of high-pressure steam was not used until much later). But instead of condensing steam in the cylinder, Watt's engine added a condenser. During the intake stroke (top) the rising piston helped to pull steam into the cylinder. During the power stroke (bottom) a valve let the steam into the condenser, where it was instantly chilled by the water-cooled walls. This caused a partial vacuum which drew the piston downwards, driving a pump arm or crankshaft.*

and stimulated commerce—and this too encouraged industrial development.

After 1760, the date commonly taken for the start of the actual Industrial Revolution, the rate of change accelerated rapidly. In the remaining 40 years of the century, the number of patents granted in England for inventions increased 10 times over, and hundreds of factories sprang up, many of them powered by James Watt's perfected steam engine. Between 1760 and 1800 life changed drastically for many thousands of people and contemporary observers knew it. "The age is running mad after innovation," Samuel Johnson said a little grumpily, "all the business of the world is to be done in a new way...." For the time being, however, the new way was in England alone: the revolution in industry did not reach the European continent until the next century.

One reason for England's head start was the abundance, in England, of "venture capital"—the availability of money at low interest rates. Most of the great factories built in England in the second half of the 18th century were built with "cheap money". But another, and more important reason was the rapid increase in the number of consumers. For a variety of interlocking reasons—better sanitation, better medical care, better and cleaner city water supplies—the population of England and Wales in the last half of the 18th century jumped from roughly 6.5 million to 9 million, an increase five times as great as that of the preceding 50 years. And some of these people were producers as well as consumers; they worked in the new factories. But the most direct source of labour for the new factories came from a revolution in agriculture.

Until about 1730 farming practices in the English countryside had changed little from those of the Middle Ages. Ploughshares were often made of wood; fields lay fallow every three years; and farm animals were slaughtered in the autumn for lack of

forage crops to carry them through the winter. Then, after 1730, following the lead of a few pioneers, the great landholders became increasingly aware that farming could be immensely profitable if done scientifically. They began to experiment with new crops, new cultivation techniques, new methods for the care and breeding of farm animals. To make these experiments economically viable, they appropriated—by the process of "enclosure" —more and more land formerly subject to communal use. Many tenant farmers, dispossessed by this manœuvre, were driven to find work in the cities.

No one, not even the most fervent admirer of the capitalistic system, can paint the Industrial Revolution as a golden age. The new manufacturers, free of legal restraints—and often of ethical ones, too—moved with ruthless confidence and in moral confusion. Uncertain whether it was wicked or good to use child labour, they did so. Able to provide men with regular work and regular pay, they seldom if ever raised wages and often set their workers a 14-, 16- and sometimes even an 18-hour day. Workers had to conform to the most rigid discipline and the punishments for those who disobeyed the rules were often harsh and brutal.

In some ways the poor suffered more intensely than before; the exploiters exploited whom they could, and there was little opportunity for redress. Beginning in 1700, when the wool-combers of Tiverton formed a friendly society that had many of the earmarks of a trade union, working men formed "combinations" for their mutual economic aid. But the middle and upper classes regarded these combinations as conspiracies and feared them as sources of mob violence. In 1799 Parliament, which had previously outlawed these associations in specific industries, outlawed them entirely. It became a criminal offence for workers to band together to improve their wages, their hours, or the employers' methods of engaging labour; it even became an offence to agitate among workers for the formation of such combinations. Thereafter, when workers organized, they had to organize clandestinely. It was not until a quarter of a century later that trade unions became legal in Great Britain.

The working classes also faced the spectre of economic dislocation. Farm workers deprived of work by the new practices and craftsmen whose skills were replaced by machines had two grim choices. They could go on relief under the Poor Law, and live in squalor on public charity in their own parishes, or they could migrate to one of the new industrial cities and live just as squalidly in one of the new urban slums. Workers repeatedly petitioned Parliament to limit the use of certain machines. When their petitions went unheard, as they frequently did, the workers attacked the source of their trouble. In the Luddite movement of 1811 to 1816, workmen rampaged against the machines they blamed for low wages or the loss of their jobs—a pathetic instance of progress claiming victims.

And yet, of course, the Industrial Revolution was also immensely beneficial. New factories brought employment to areas long sunk in economic stagnation. And the new machines, brutalizing as they were, did give regular work to many labourers who had been only casually or occasionally employed. These were only the immediate, obvious benefits. The greatest benefit of all, unseen at the time, was the Industrial Revolution's *laissez-faire* philosophy, which treated men as adults rather than as wards of the State or cogs in a military machine. This mass coming-of-age of a whole stratum of society liberated energies that prepared the way for the enormous expansion of Western economic life that is still going on today.

One philosophy in particular seemed to contain within itself all the varying strands of the Enlightenment. Its name was Utilitarianism. Like a num-

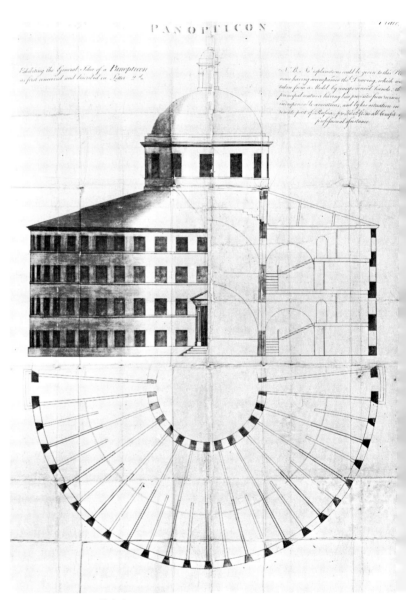

A MODEL PRISON *called the Panopticon was designed by reformer Jeremy Bentham "to grind rogues honest and idle men industrious". It was never built, but its circular concept, in which a central guard could supervise all outside cells, influenced prison architecture.*

ber of other Enlightenment ideas it was based on an ancient Greek philosophy, Epicureanism. From Epicurean doctrine—that men by nature seek pleasure and avoid pain—the Utilitarians developed the theory that societies should be so organized that pleasure is distributed through them as widely as possible. The slogan of the Utilitarians was "the greatest good for the greatest number", and the man who argued this principle most insistently and most persuasively was Jeremy Bentham, the movement's founder.

Although Bentham's teachings did not come into their own until the 19th century, he himself was very much a product of the 18th century. Not only was he born into it, in 1748, but he was reared by it according to the tenets of Enlightenment philosophy. His father, a lawyer, ambitiously intended his son for the office of Lord Chancellor. Bentham was studying Latin grammar at 4, and Latin composition at 5; at 13, he entered Oxford. He went on to study law, but was very unhappy in this career. He thought that most of England's troubles resulted from its blind and foolish laws. Consequently he retired from active practice as soon as he was able to, and devoted his time to schemes for improving not only English law but the entire structure of English government.

Bentham was not a man to readily acknowledge his indebtedness to other men; nevertheless he owes something to several other philosophers of the Enlightenment. Like David Hume, he was a sceptic; he had no patience with philosophical fictions, objecting to such devices as Rousseau's "social contract", a theory which he said had no basis in historical fact. He was also indebted to Voltaire for his anticlericalism, and for his humanitarian concern with judicial reforms. To another French *philosophe*, Claude Adrien Helvétius, Bentham owed one of the key ideas of his Utilitarian philosophy—the usefulness of man's instinctive pursuit of happiness. In his controversial book *Concerning the Mind*, Helvétius had argued that man at birth is a blank slate; he is a product of his education and environment. Claiming that man's only motive for action was self-interest, Helvétius said that it followed that man could be indoctrinated with any idea simply by using a system of rewards and punishments—in other words, pleasure and pain. (One critic observed—half in anger, half in amusement—that Helvétius was only saying what everyone had always known to be true, but never said out loud.)

Bentham combined these different strands of thought into an aggressive philosophy. He spent his long life attempting to discredit the psychological, legal and political fictions that kept men from realizing their potential for happiness. In pursuit of this aim he sometimes became obsessed by odd causes, and was perhaps a little mad. But his influence always favoured sanity. He is credited, for example, with spurring reforms in the English prison system, although one of his proposals—for a model prison called a Panopticon—seems more curious than corrective. The Panopticon would have been a building so designed that the inmates would be under constant surveillance. They would not be maltreated, but they would be conditioned to recognize the pain that resulted from anti-social acts and the pleasure that came from virtuous ones. It was a scheme at once horrible and humane.

But such eccentricities do not touch the heart of Bentham's thought and influence—an influence that brought about reforms in the English legal system, in the English government and in almost every other aspect of English life. He is credited with contributing to the mitigation of the terrible criminal laws, the removal of defects in the jury system, the abolition of imprisonment for debt, the sweeping away of usury laws. He brought about reforms in the representative system of Parliament, advocated the repeal of religious tests as a prerequisite to public office, and urged the establishment of a national system of education. He extended the idea of savings banks, cheap postage and the institution of postal money orders. He proposed a uniform registry for population statistics, a registry of real estate, a wider circulation of Parliamentary papers, legal protection for inventors, and the passage of public health laws.

It is a formidable list, and a strange one. Bentham could be equally obsessive about great issues like Parliamentary reforms and small matters like postal money orders. But it was always an obsession that fitted his philosophical preoccupation with the perfectibility of man and society. The world as it was, the real world, Bentham seemed to say, could be adjusted to become the world that ought to be, the ideal world. The key to the adjustment was man's recognition of the nature and value of his pleasure under any given circumstance. To aid in this evaluation, Bentham invented what he called the "felicific calculus", a system which men could use to measure scientifically the attributes of pleasure—its intensity, duration, certainty, propinquity, fecundity, purity and extent.

Whatever the scientific validity of this calculus, and however odd Bentham may sound, his reforming philosophy was solidly based on a thoroughly respectable scientific idea: the utility of the principles of pleasure and pain. "Nature has placed mankind under the governance of two sovereign masters, pain and pleasure", begins one of his most important works, *An Introduction to the Principles of Morals and Legislation*. "It is for them alone to point out what we ought to do, as well as to determine what we shall do. On the one hand the standard of right and wrong, on the other the chain of causes and effects, are fastened to their throne."

It has often been argued that Bentham was confused. If, as he contended, pleasure both should and did guide men, then what need was there for thought, or moral reflection—or even of Bentham's own work? In fact he was expressing a complex inner tension in simple terms—and this tension lies at the heart of his philosophical position. Men seek pleasure, and rightly so. But the pleasures they seek are often deceptive, temporary and irrational. Men need to examine and be clear about the precise quality of their pleasure. Debauchery, for instance, may offer some immediate joy but in the long run its result is pain—to seek such pleasure is childish and irrational. On the other hand, to yearn for pleasure, and to fail to gratify oneself out of some ascetic notion of self-sacrifice, is also wrong. To deny oneself pleasure for such reasons results in a life of grim inner conflicts and perpetual discomfort.

One vicious force that stood in the way of men's pursuit of pleasure, said Bentham, was the self-interest of their rulers. Another was religion, which throughout history had kept men in subjection to false, destructive ideals. Not even philosophy, he said, had guided men as it should, for until his own time it had simply been the intellectual plaything of the few. Consequently there was an enormous gap between the pleasure men actually sought, in their ignorance, and the pleasure they might seek if they were permitted to be enlightened. Bentham saw two ways to close this gap. First, he would educate men: help them to reason and thus to calculate the consequences of their actions, help them to see the nonsense in much of what passed for philosophy. Secondly, he would tear down the institutions—religious, political, social—that deprived men of the chance to realize themselves as rational, pleasure-seeking beings.

Education and social reform thus went hand in hand, and Bentham's Utilitarianism, crude and naïve and philistine, was also immensely beneficial and immensely profound. It put the moral sciences at the service of all mankind.

NEWLY RICH *after his father's death, ne'er-do-well Tom Rakewell is measured for a suit as a mother confronts him with the daughter he seduced.*

# RAKES AND RIBALDRY

In England the Enlightenment's veneer of elegance and reason lightly cloaked a lusty era of change. Land and high birth, traditional hallmarks of prestige, were yielding ground to the growing force of hard, ready cash. In London's teeming confusion, sons of smugglers and bootblacks found the way to wealth and rank. It was an age of optimism and, inevitably, excess. When Parliament passed a temperance law, mobs took to the streets, crying "No gin, no King!" Of all contemporary commentators, no one cast a more satiric eye on this seamy side of England than the artist William Hogarth, whose set of paintings *The Rake's Progress* traces a young nitwit's fall from wealth to debauchery, debt and insanity.

A FLOCK OF FRAUDS *seeking Rakewell's patronage surrounds him in his London house. A dancing master poses, a gardener presents landscape plans, and a jockey holds a silver bowl won in a horse race.*

# A TASTE FOR
# FOPPERY AND GIN

Young spendthrifts in 18th-century London attracted two types of parasites. Culture peddlers catered to the rich Englishman's passion for tasteless ornamentation and *exotica* by providing, for a fee, everything from bad French and Italian art to music and dancing lessons. More to Tom Rakewell's liking were the wenches, drinkers and gamblers who haunted London's innumerable taverns. In these raucous citadels of the city's low life the chief attraction was gin—in the first part of the century gin consumption rose more than tenfold in England—and there was plenty of evidence to support Lord Chesterfield's complaint in Parliament that "this liquor corrupts the mind, enervates the body . . . and destroys vigour and virtue at the same time".

A SPREE IN A TAVERN *leaves the Rake in a stupor at 3 o'clock in the morning after a night of drinking and rioting; two of the women collaborate in stealing his watch. At his feet lie souvenirs of the evening's mischief, a watchman's staff and lantern. A famous grog-house slogan of Hogarth's time was "Drunk for a Penny, Dead Drunk for Twopence and Clean Straw for Nothing".*

ARRESTED FOR DEBT, *the Rake is stopped by two bailiffs. Only a prompt payment made by his forsaken sweetheart (right) saves him from prison.*

# A BAD TIME FOR DEBTORS

Wealth increased prodigiously in 18th-century England. The commercial revolution brought up from the lower economic orders a new moneyed class whose fortunes rested on trade rather than the soil. Merchants like Tom Rakewell's father begot "gentlemen" sons whose doltish mentality could not be obscured by their ostentation. The centre of this social upheaval was London, a boom town of quick profit and quicker loss, a place where a Rakewell could easily forfeit his entire patrimony at the gaming table and end up deep in debt.

MARRYING FOR MONEY, *Tom takes a pop-eyed, hunchbacked crone to wife in a quick ceremony conducted by a clergyman as corrupt as the couple.*

Although glittering mansions were rising to house urbanized aristocrats and merchants, London remained a city of dirt, disease and crime. Along the dimly lit streets footpads and pickpockets flourished. Over the roof-tops hung a thick haze darkened by coal fumes. Bad air was not the only peril: smallpox alone killed 1 in 13 and in 1740 London burials outnumbered baptisms 2 to 1.

Life was thought cheap, cheaper than goods, and crimes against property were savagely punished. At least 150 transgressions carried the death penalty; men might hang for the theft of a rabbit (though juries were usually reluctant to apply the full weight of the law). Debt, though not a hanging offence, was a serious one. A debtor like Tom might be accosted on the street by a bailiff and whisked off to prison to languish for years, deprived of any chance to make repayment. It is not surprising that Tom was prepared to go to any lengths to cheat the jailer. When he wed a rich old shrew, avarice was not his only motive—his freedom was at stake.

# GAMBLING ON THE ROAD TO HELL

The favourite indoor sport of 18th-century England was gambling. Stakes were high. At London taverns like White's (*below*), where Tom is seen back at his old tricks, the pot could mount as high as £100,000. Beau Nash, the colourful master of ceremonies at the fashionable resort of Bath, often won whole inheritances from spendthrift rakes—though sometimes he was known to return his winnings with a warning. Usually, heavy losses meant debt and debt meant prison—as Rakewell discovered.

The prisons, crowded and disease-ridden, were a lucrative business for jailers. Prisoners with any money had to pay for food and lodgings. Juvenile offenders, petty thieves and debtors were packed in together with murderers and the insane. In a day when public hangings at Tyburn drew enthusiastic crowds and when heads of traitors were left to rot in the public view, barbarity was common among jailers. Henry Fielding, novelist and magistrate, called England's prisons "the prototype of hell"

RUINED BY GAMBLING, *the last of his money gone, the Rake tears off his wig and kneels in despair. Behind him other gamesters count up their winnings as the dice game goes on. The scene is White's Chocolate House, frequented by most of the day's famous men.*

IMPRISONED FOR DEBT, *Rakewell is dunned by an urchin for money to pay for a mug of beer, while his wife scolds and the jailer insists on his tip. On the table is a manuscript of a play, rejected by a publisher, with which Rakewell hoped to redeem his fortunes.*

# A BITTER END
# IN BEDLAM

The final stage in the Rake's sad descent
was the horror of Bedlam, a London insane
asylum whose name, a corruption of Beth-
lehem Hospital, has stayed in the language
as a synonym for chaos. On quiet nights
the noise of the confined lunatics "rattling
their chains and making terrible out-cry"
echoed across the city. During the day the
inmates were on view for curious London
sightseers, who paid to walk around the
grounds enjoying the antics of the mad.

Bedlam's patients elicited little compassion, since it was widely believed that the
mentally afflicted were not only incurable
but insensitive to hunger, thirst, cold and
pain. Thus they were ill fed, ill clothed
and cruelly treated. Hogarth's "Scene in
Bedlam" captures the horror of the place.
The Rake, removed from prison after trying to commit suicide, lies naked on the
straw. While two fashionable ladies look
on curiously (*left, centre*), the woman
Rakewell discarded, still faithful, kneels
beside him. But the dissolute chronicle
of Tom Rakewell has come to a bitter end.

# 6
# MEN OF MUSIC

MOZART'S CLAVICHORD, *carefully preserved in his house in Salzburg, recalls both the graceful music and the bareness of the composer's final years. His unfinished portrait, painted by a relative, hangs above it on the wall.*

"Pushpin", said the 18th-century sociologist Jeremy Bentham, "is as good as poetry." He was not trying to suggest that the children's game was as noble as a sonnet. Rather, he thought that the pleasure derived from them could be equal, and therefore—in a society that provided the greatest good for the greatest number—one was as good as the other. Sometimes, in their eagerness for social improvement, the men of the Enlightenment sounded like Philistines.

Still, they did not forget to cultivate the arts. Voltaire could write angry essays attacking judicial injustice, but *Candide*—whatever else it may be—is undoubtedly a literary masterpiece. Lessing's earnest dialogues on behalf of tolerance may read like tracts, but his tragedies and comedies were splendid dramas, fine enough to remain in production to this day. And in one art the 18th century reached heights matched by few other ages, before or after. In music the century of the Enlightenment was truly a great century.

Music is the most abstract of arts. Its connection with the social and political climate of its time is not easy to establish. Many of the greatest 18th-century composers never suffered a moment's religious doubt, even though they lived in the midst of an age of religious questioning. Yet there were close ties between music and the Enlightenment. The composers of the age shared the ferment of their day, and created great music in part because they were surrounded, in the world of culture and art, by men of innovation.

In the early 18th century, musical innovation reached into every branch of the art, vocal and instrumental, and brought enormous changes to every kind of musical composition. Composers of this period, the late Baroque, combined instruments and voice in a profusion of ways, and typically labelled their compositions with what today seems a happy confusion of names. Vivaldi and Scarlatti, Telemann and Couperin, Buxtehude and Croelli entitled their compositions *concerto*, *sinfonia* and *sonata*, but the terms had no fixed meaning. Sonata, for example, was a name that applied equally to a composition for a single instrument, a few instruments or even a small orchestra.

Yet, for all this loose titling of works, Baroque

THE ART OF THE MINUET *depended on stately, measured steps, performed with the utmost grace and control. This was a necessary skill for every gentleman and lady of the Enlightenment. Basic steps and accompanying hand motions are shown on the right. The minuet's popularity drew many composers to write music for it; it even worked its way into the symphonies of Haydn and Mozart.*

composers developed brilliant musical forms. And two Baroque composers explored these formal elements with a special profundity and skill. Neither Bach nor Handel was an innovator, but both were superb technicians and both were musical geniuses. Their mastery of existing forms closed one musical age and opened the door on another, paving the way for the three great composers of the Enlightenment: Gluck, Haydn and Mozart.

Johann Sebastian Bach's life was uneventful except for his music—and in his own lifetime he was not even especially famous for that. People knew him as an enormously gifted organist, but the range and power of his talent as a composer went unheralded and unsung except among other musicians.

Bach was born into a large and musical family in 1685, fathered 20 children of his own, and lived out his life as an organist and music master in the petty courts and provincial towns of Germany. But if the externals of his life were routine, his passion for music was extraordinary and he never stopped exploring it. He went on pilgrimages to hear the leading musicians of his day, such as Buxtehude in Lübeck, and twice he set out in pursuit of Handel —although they never met. He copied out whatever music came into his hands, not from a want of inspiration but because he wanted to understand what inspired other men. He studied the Italians, who had broken away from traditional polyphonic music and were writing in new combinations of harmonies and instrumental textures; he studied the French, who were composing keyboard suites based on the measures of the dance. He became a superb organist and taught himself to play the violin. And he incorporated all that he learned into his own musical compositions.

Bach's output as a composer is as impressive in quantity as it is superb in quality. He wrote secular music and church music; cantatas and chorales; concertos and suites; solo pieces for the organ, harpsichord and clavichord, the violin, the flute and the cello. He even wrote fingering exercises for his students (among whom were several of his own children who eventually became well-known musicians in their own right).

His secular music often reflects his love of life and boisterous humour—witness the *Coffee Cantata*, a musical dialogue between a girl and her father over whether it was quite proper for a girl to drink that exciting new beverage, coffee. But sometimes his music is meant as a lesson. *The Well-Tempered Clavier*, a series of 48 pairs of preludes and fugues, written in every possible key, expressed Bach's belief in a then-new practice of tempering—or tuning—the keyboard so that the octave was divided into 12 equal parts. The tempered keyboard permitted keyboard music to be played in every possible key, and greatly extended the versatility of the instrument. Similarly, the *Art of the Fugue* explored counterpoint and the possibilities of the fugue beyond anything that had ever been tried before, and is considered by many music lovers to be the pinnacle of this musical form.

But Bach's true musical vocation was neither teaching nor entertaining; it was the service of God. Whether he was setting music to words or labouring over the intricacies of the harpsichord, his motives were deeply religious. The goal of such "mighty fortresses" as the *Mass in B Minor* and *St. Matthew Passion* was to achieve, in Bach's words, "well-ordered music in the honour of God"—well ordered that is, in technical craftsmanship, and musically clear, because God himself was the Great Craftsman, to be honoured as much by good works as by prayer. With this idea, so essentially Lutheran, Bach placed himself spiritually in the heart of the Reformation and musically summed up an age. "Music owes as much to Bach", said Robert Schumann a century later, "as religion owes to its founder."

122

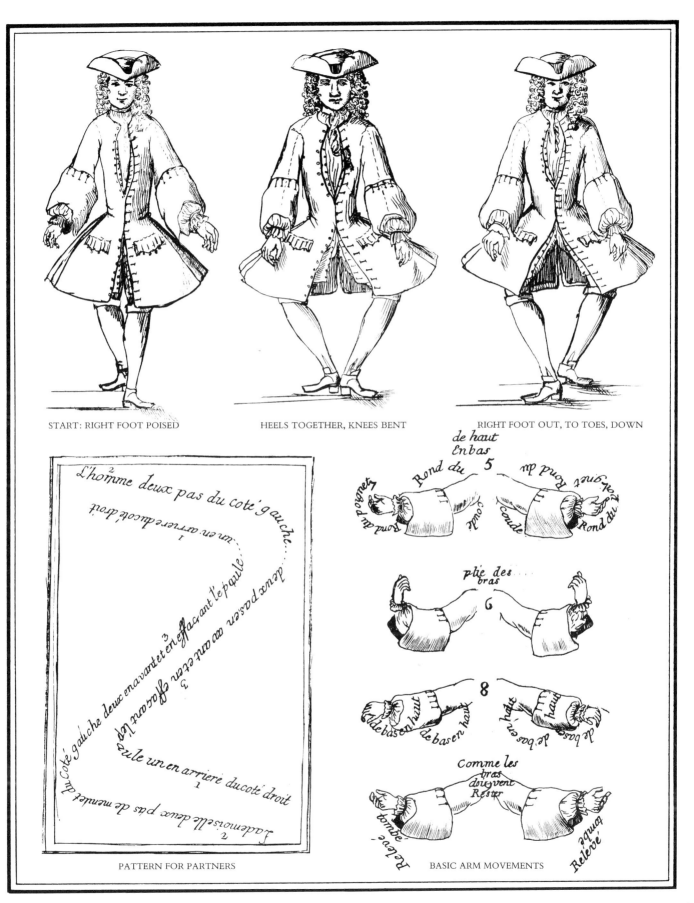

START: RIGHT FOOT POISED

HEELS TOGETHER, KNEES BENT

RIGHT FOOT OUT, TO TOES, DOWN

PATTERN FOR PARTNERS

BASIC ARM MOVEMENTS

AN ACADEMY OF SCIENCE *in St. Peters-burg contained a library stocked with thousands of technical treatises. It was the great German philosopher Gottfried Leibnitz who persuaded Peter the Great to found the Academy. But when it opened in 1725, no Russians could pass the entrance tests, and eight students had to be imported from Germany.*

Перспективной видъ Библиоте-кй втораго и третяго апарта-ментовъ. | Perspectivischer aufriß von der Bibliothec des zweiten und dritten Stockwerks. | Prospect de la Bibliotheque qui est au second et troisieme Etage. | Sciagraphia penetralium Biblio-thecæ in secunda et tertia conti-gnatione.

revolutionary. Instead of being rebels the early *Aufklärer* were literally and figuratively academics: Christian Thomasius and Christian Wolff were university professors who taught enlightened ideas, but they enlightened without losing the support of respectable, responsible men; Johann Christoph Gottsched was a vigorous literary critic, but his criticism was more concerned with the rules of literature than with its inner life.

It is easier to disparage these men for their pedantry than to give them their just due. Thomasius tried to set German thought on its own feet by lecturing in German—an unprecedented action in the stilted scholastic world of the German university. And like the French *philosophes*, he battled against belief in witchcraft and the use of torture in courts. Similarly, Wolff—also lecturing in German, rather than Latin—made Leibnitz's rational Christianity, and rational philosophy in general, as popular as theology among civilized Germans.

Even Gottsched, for all his preoccupation with literary rules, deserves credit for being more than a dry academician. In his literary periodicals and his books, Gottsched laboured mightily to elevate the German theatre above the crude Punch and Judy shows that for years had been its standard fare. He held up to his readers as an ideal the classical theatre of France, and suggested that by selective and intelligent imitation Germany could achieve both cultural growth and cultural independence. "What the Greeks were to the Romans," he told his readers, "the French are to us."

By the middle of the 18th century, educated Germans were ready to move beyond Gottsched's prescriptions to Gottsched's goal. A small troop of literary men began to pour out German poems and plays. Most of these men are now forgotten, but one of them, Gotthold Ephraim Lessing, through his noble spirit and interesting mind, has entered world literature.

Lessing was born in 1729, the son of a well-educated but impecunious Saxon pastor. He devoured the Greek and Roman classics early, and gradually, painfully abandoned the faith of his fathers. Starting from orthodox Lutheranism, he went to rationalist Lutheranism, then to deism and finally to a highly individualistic religious philosophy of his own. It was a philosophy at once hostile to orthodox Christianity and critical of the religious rationalism of the German Enlightenment. The *Aufklärer*, with their contempt for the historical significance of the Christian story, annoyed him; orthodox Christians, with their credulous piety and their refusal to let their minds range freely over their beliefs, were unacceptable to him.

Lessing believed that religion was neither a thing to be ridiculed nor a thing to be followed blindly. The religious impulse, he said, existed in all men—had existed long before there were theologies to serve it and would continue to exist if theologies should cease. But religion evolved, as men evolved. From primitive beliefs based on superstition and magic, it advanced to beliefs that arrived at a sense of God through mystical communion. Lessing's concept of religion as an evolutionary process—as both being and becoming—explained some of the apparent discrepancies in Biblical morality that bothered the 18th century. It made Biblical heroes like David, for instance—men who were supposed to be paragons of wisdom and goodness, but who actually were not—easier to understand and accept.

But however much Lessing disagreed with his fellow *Aufklärer* on some points, he was one of them in spirit, for he was above all a critic. In fact Lessing himself, knowing his own strengths and weaknesses, candidly described himself as a talented critic rather than a creative genius. The most important of his critical studies was probably *Laocoön*, an essay which uses the famous Greek statue to argue a point in aesthetics: should all art forms treat their subject in the same manner? Traditionally the answer to this question was yes; painting was silent poetry, poetry was spoken painting. But Lessing disagreed. Some arts, he said, were concerned with space, while others were concerned with time, and this made a difference in the artist's approach to his subject.

The arts of space—painting and sculpture—perpetuate a single moment in time, and their beauty paradoxically was therefore to be judged on their timelessness. If Laocoön, wrestling with the serpent for the lives of his sons, had been shown with his face as intensely contorted as the moment truly demanded, the statue would have been less effective as art. Pain ends, but Laocoön's pain, caught in marble, would go on for ever—becoming less profound, because less real, each time one looked at it. Poetry, on the other hand, said Lessing, exists in time. It deals not with a single moment but with the whole of transitory events; the beauty of poetry is that it traces an event—even an emotional event like Laocoön's agony—from beginning to end.

Today aesthetic tastes have changed, and Lessing's distinctions between the arts are mainly of historical importance. But in his own time they liberated writers and painters alike, unleashing them from dogmatic rules which limited their inventiveness and spontaneity.

Similarly, in another important critical work, a series of short essays published as the *Hamburg Dramaturgy*, Lessing brought new life to the theatre. Vigorously, effectively—and sometimes a little harshly—he condemned classical French drama, with its artificial rules, and praised the freely constructed dramas of Shakespeare and the popular dramas of Diderot. In fact, he did more than criticize; he constructed plays of his own. At first he simply offered German audiences a taste of the realism which he so much admired in English and French popular dramas. But in his two masterpieces, *Minna von*

*Barnhelm* and *Nathan the Wise*, Lessing almost singlehandedly created the modern German theatre.

*Minna von Barnhelm*, published in 1767, is a comedy about a young Saxon noblewoman who gently pursues and finally captures a proud but diffident Prussian army officer who thinks he cannot marry her because his name has been dishonoured. Its characters are drawn from contemporary German life, and its reconciled lovers seemed especially poignant to German audiences, for Prussia and Saxony had recently fought on opposing sides in the Seven Years' War. Today *Minna von Barnhelm* is chiefly important because it was the first truly German version of the sentimental bourgeois play.

*Nathan the Wise*, which followed it in 1779, is also a play about reconciliation—but on the highest possible level; it is a play about religious tolerance. Nathan, its chief character, is an old and wise Jew who has lived a life of bitter experience and gleaned from it a humane philosophy. With reasonable argument and the use of touching allegory, he overcomes the stubborn prejudices of a Christian and a Moslem. In the end all three agree that all the great religions of man are alike in essence, for all teach the true faith—the brotherhood of man.

Although Lessing fought to free his own German culture from its dependence on foreign models, *Nathan the Wise* shows him to be far more than merely a German nationalist, and shows the *Aufklärung* to be far more than merely a parochial revolt. At its best the German Enlightenment was an attempt to join and extend the cultures of other nations. Three other great *Aufklärer*, each in his own way, also reflect this attempt.

The first of the three was Johann Joachim Winckelmann, Lessing's contemporary and the inspiration for his *Laocoön*. Winckelmann was a poverty-stricken German scholar who conceived an overwhelming passion for ancient Greece—especially its sculpture—and made a cult of its noble simplicity

MEANWHILE, IN JAPAN . . .

An Orientalized Dutch trader living in Japan smokes his clay pipe—thinking perhaps about that country's restrictions on foreign trade. For while Europe was lightening, Japan was dark. Fearing Western ways and missionary interference, the nation had virtually closed all doors to foreigners since the early 17th century. A handful of Dutch traders who remained were confined to a tiny island in Nagasaki Bay. But individual Japanese continued to be fascinated with Western technology and thought; scholars plied the lonely Dutch with questions about Western medicine, astronomy, botany and the new wonders of electricity, and gradually established Western libraries and schools. In 1853 U.S. Commodore Matthew Perry arrived in Tokyo with a fleet, and re-established contact between the two worlds.

and quiet grandeur. This virtual elevation of art into the realm of religion created an aesthetic bridge across which 18th-century Germany could move to explore the ideals of pagan Greece. The insights that Winckelmann provided, coupled with the international debates his writings caused, helped to link German theories about aesthetics to similar theories in England and France.

Christoph Martin Wieland, the second of the *Aufklärer* to attempt a synthesis of several cultural strains, was as much a lover of classical beauty as Winckelmann. But where Winckelmann's genius was tormented, and his attention largely riveted upon an ideal of male beauty, Wieland concentrated more on the sensuality of the ancient Greeks, and was himself a great pursuer of woman. It is no accident that he devoted much time to translating Cicero and Lucian, whose works were more influenced by Hellenistic than Classical Greece, and no accident that his own piquant novels are set in Hellenistic times.

Wieland's message was worldly wisdom; he accepted both reason and the senses, and preached the tranquil enjoyment of life. He was a sensualist who saw no evil in sex; a cosmopolitan who learned much from Voltaire about wit and style, and, at the same time, admired and translated Shakespeare; and he was a secularist who made gentle fun of religion and sharp fun of superstition. When the German Romantics came to power a generation later, Wieland was downgraded for his Frenchified frivolity—an unfair judgement, for his essays are still read as models of good sense, and his urbane tales and poems still make pleasant reading.

Compared to the fantasies and lighthearted ironies of Wieland, the philosophizing of Immanuel Kant seems austere indeed. Yet he too, like Winckelmann and Wieland, was attempting to fuse the different elements of French, English and German thought, and he was a good deal more of a cosmo-

politan than he is normally given credit for being. Popular legend has turned Kant into a rigid pedant; it has been said of him that he took his daily walks so punctually that the housewives of Königsberg set their clocks by him. Actually he was a witty conversationalist and a delightful dinner companion. One of his students, Johann Herder, described him as a man who "in his most vigorous manhood had the gay liveliness of a youth which will, I believe, accompany him into his old age. His forehead, built for thinking, was the seat of indestructible serenity and joy, talk rich in ideas issued from his lips, joking, humour and wit were at his disposal, and his teaching lectures were the most amusing concourse".

Kant began his philosophical studies along the lines laid down by the *Aufklärer* Christian Wolff, who believed that man could discover the laws of nature through rational inquiry—by observing cause and effect, and drawing logical deductions. But Kant rejected Wolff's doctrinaire certainties when he came in contact with the sceptical writings of Hume, for Hume showed him that the relationship between cause and effect could never be proved, only assumed. Similarly, he was influenced by Rousseau. Absorbing Rousseau's belief in the innate goodness of man, he came to believe that ethical and moral values, far from being acquired, were intrinsic to man's nature.

From the insights gained through these studies Kant constructed his three great *Critiques*—of pure reason, of practical reason and of judgement. They are critical books, but critical in the deepest sense: they are searching and severe examinations of three important realms of philosophy—metaphysics, ethics and aesthetics. Kant himself said that he was trying to write a philosophy of philosophy, a system of knowledge that included and went beyond all other systems. When reasonable men spoke of what they "knew", what were they actually entitled to say? How far could reason be depended upon? Was there a point past which reason could not go?

Kant's investigation of the nature of knowledge was an enterprise in the great tradition of Newton and Hume. Like Newton, whose motto was that he did not invent hypotheses, Kant took actual experience as his philosophical starting point. Like Hume, he was sceptical of all sensory "proofs" of knowledge. But unlike Hume, he did not intend the outcome of his study to be sceptical. Kant believed that the mind was not simply a passive receptacle for sensory information, but that it evaluated and interpreted sense impressions. It did this through categories of perception, inherent in the very structure of the mind. Probably the most famous of these was the "categorical imperative", a sort of philosophical version of the Golden Rule: it held that the behaviour of man was dictated by an intuitive standard which prompted him to act as he thought other men should act.

The influence of Kant was wide and deep. His mind ranged over so many fields and illuminated so many matters that Goethe (whose mind was almost as various) said that reading him was like entering a lighted room. Yet even as Kant wrote, his ideas were being challenged for the attention of the German public by another, more emotional stream of thought. And this new element was jeopardizing the achievements of the German Enlightenment. It came to be called *Sturm und Drang*, Storm and Stress, after a melodramatic play by Friedrich Klinger that typified the movement.

*Sturm und Drang* was a rebellious movement of young German intellectuals against the Enlightenment's prevailing mood of optimism, which to them seemed unjustified. They thought society far from perfect. Most of the young men who carried its banners burned out early; their plays and poetry, full of overblown emotions, are remembered today only by specialists. Also, with their worship of the titan and the tough guy, the *Kraftkerl*, they voiced a morbid strain in German thought that was to reappear tragically in later German history.

Nevertheless, *Sturm und Drang* was not wholly unhealthy. It did point to a defect in the German Enlightenment—its complacent rationalism. And it did raise some important questions about aesthetics. Instead of following the classical rules for art and the classical models, the young men of *Sturm und Drang* proclaimed virtues of an art that followed nature and extolled imagination, intuition and "genius". They believed in being free—it might be disorderly but it was exciting. Also the movement did enlist, at least for a time, some of the most talented poets and thinkers of the day. There was Johann Herder, who believed in folk cultures—Hebrew, Irish, Baltic, Slavic, as well as German—and encouraged the young Goethe to go out into the countryside and collect the songs of the people. There was Friedrich Schiller, whose youthful melodramas—*The Robbers*, *Fiasco* and *Intrigue and Love*—denounced the established order and thrilled their audiences. And finally, there was the young Goethe.

Goethe is the best known and least imitated of all German literary figures. His achievements as a writer and as a man were so gigantic and so many-sided that admirers read him with awe, quoted him constantly, but elevated him to heights that made him impossible to follow. Part of his long life (1749-1832) goes beyond the Age of Enlightenment into the Romantic Age. But his talents ripened early and allowed him to dominate the cultural scene of the last decades of 18th-century Germany.

Goethe appears to be a man of Olympian poise, but the appearance deceives. He was, as he said himself, a chameleon, a man of many moods; the poise is the product of hard work and clever disguise. After a time of feverish creation he would lapse into indolence, throughout his life undergoing alternate periods of depression and renewal.

He was also a chameleon in the dazzling variety of his activities. He was an imaginative and somewhat erratic natural scientist, pursuing the study of geology, anatomy and optics—although his interest in these subjects stemmed partly from his need for a link with the world of things. He was a gifted and appreciative translator of writers as diverse as the *philosophe* Diderot, the romantic poet Lord Byron and the flamboyant artist Benvenuto Cellini. Besides this, he was an intelligent and important literary critic, a perceptive autobiographer, a fine talker, and a poet of great lyrical beauty. Most important, he was an immensely influential novelist and playwright.

The best of Goethe's works during the period of his association with the *Sturm und Drang* movement is the *Sorrows of Young Werther*, a novel that explores the morbid sensibilities of adolescence with penetrating skill (although, unfortunately, in poor translation it reads like a sentimental love story). Werther is a young man completely absorbed in his own feelings. He falls in love with a girl, Lotte, but soon realizes he cannot have her. He leaves, leads a wandering life, and eventually kills himself.

*Werther* was such a success that young German intellectuals affected dress à la Werther—sky-blue coat, yellow breeches, jackboots—and committed enough Werther-inspired suicides to prompt Goethe to add a cautionary introduction to the novel's second edition.

Two decades after *Werther*, Goethe published a second important novel, *Wilhelm Meister's Apprenticeship*, a book that became the model for what came to be called the *Bildungsroman*, in effect, "portrait novel". It depicts the growth of a young man, through experience, to maturity. Unlike *Werther*, its central character wants to live in the real world as well as the interior world of his own senses, and the story of the novel is Wilhelm Meister's gradual adjustment of his own goals to the goals of society.

The last of Goethe's great novels is the grave and mysterious *Elective Affinities*, a story that explores the conflict between the man-made ideal of marital fidelity and the natural attraction of men and women for each other which destroys the most sacred social bond. "In it," said Goethe (who perpetually contended in his own life with the same problem), "I have deposited with deep emotion many a sad experience." The book tells the story of Edward and Charlotte, man and wife; a captain, who is Edward's best friend; and Ottilie, Charlotte's stepdaughter. Edward and Ottilie fall in love, as do Charlotte and the captain, but Edward and Ottilie give in to their passion while Charlotte and the captain restrain themselves out of a sense of duty. Both love stories are presented with compassion, but Goethe nevertheless takes sides: Edward and Ottilie, exhausted by their emotions, waste away and die.

In his plays Goethe roamed all over the known dramatic map, and discovered some new territories of his own. *Götz von Berlichingen*, written in the early 1770's when he was still young and under the influence of *Sturm und Drang*, is a vigorous imitation of Shakespeare. It is full of vitality and disorder, rich in colourful characters and in high and low speech. Its hero is a real person, a 16th-century robber baron who in Goethe's play becomes a sort of Robin Hood. Young Götz rebels against the artificial conventions of society and joins the peasants in their fight against oppression. He dies of wounds, with a cry of freedom on his lips. The style of *Götz* was almost completely put aside in the later plays. *Iphigenia in Taurus* and *Torquato Tasso* are profoundly classical in their inwardness, their few characters, their restrained language and lack of violent action. *Iphigenia* is written in the measured calm of blank verse and devotes itself

to the theme of guilt and expiation. Unlike their Greek originals, however, the characters in Goethe's play are not pawns of the gods, but real individuals, discovering guilt and forgiveness for themselves. Similarly, in *Tasso*, Goethe explores the private hell of the 16th-century Italian poet —and by inference the terrifying plight of any talented but neurotic artist who cannot function in the world in which we lives.

And then there is *Faust*, the play that everyone half knows—a sprawling, complex work that is literally and figuratively torn in two. Part One, the familiar part, is relatively simple. It tells of the young scholar Faust's pact with the Devil, who promises him happiness in return for his soul, and of Faust's seduction of Gretchen, which ultimately results in her madness and death. Part Two, much more richly textured, is so completely different from Part One that it seems alien to it. In it the mature Faust ventures out into a larger, symbolic world. The Devil allows him to know supreme beauty in a marriage with Helen of Troy, and worldly success as the sole ruler of a virgin tract of land which he colonizes according to his idea of the perfect State. But both are won through force and trickery. In the end, however, Faust finds a welcome in heaven—partly through his own ceaseless striving to improve his actions, partly through the help of a supernatural love.

This catalogue of Goethe's achievements, for all its length, is far from complete, but it shows how difficult it is to fit him into any one cultural category. The Germans have solved the problem by giving him an age of his own. The decades in which he had his greatest influence, at the end of the 18th century and the beginning of the 19th century, are, they say, *Goethezeit*—a time superior in colour and depth and understanding to the "shallow Enlightenment". There is some justice for this view. Goethe's range of interests, his wisdom, his cosmopolitan grasp of many cultures make Diderot's versatility, Wieland's good sense, and Lessing's humanity seem pale by comparison.

But Goethe was not in every way the culminating figure of the 18th century. For one thing, he had little sympathy with the political revolution implicit in the ideas of the English and French Enlightenments. He believed in individual freedom —his own. And he interpreted it as freedom to search for his own perfection. When he went from his native Frankfurt to the little State of Weimar, in 1775, at the invitation of its youthful and generous duke, Karl August, he went because the duke's invitation seemed to offer him freedom of creativity. When he ran away to Italy 11 years later, again in search of freedom, it was to escape from the influence of his beloved Charlotte von Stein. Goethe's belief in freedom was personal rather than social, and in this sense he left German culture no better than he found it. In fact he even strengthened the political docility of his readers by holding up to them an ideal more concerned with the perfection of self than with the perfection of society. A man's ability to live to the full was to be achieved not at the barricades but in contemplation—an unfortunate departure from the realistic radicalism of the *philosophes.*

In fairness to Goethe it is also important to add that in one way he fulfilled the Enlightenment: in an age of criticism, he was the epitome of the critic. Goethe gazed with cool disillusion upon all traditional religious beliefs and intellectual convictions. His own ambiguous attitude towards Christianity included an appreciation of its historical role and a delight in the dramatic possibilities of the Christian myth. But in general he looked upon all religion as a metaphorical explanation for the mysterious workings of the universe.

In this sense Goethe was no stranger to reverence. But he was, as he said more than once and

in various ways, "decidedly a non-Christian". He admired the wonders of the universe and went along with the deists' view of God as the Divine Watchmaker of an intricately beautiful world. Like the *philosophes*, he was a pagan. But where they took their paganism from the morality of Rome, Goethe went back for his to the sunny sensuality of Greece, discovering it first indirectly through Winckelmann, then later for himself in his journeys through Italy, the "land where the lemon trees bloom". To Goethe the doctrine of original sin was not only alien; it was repugnant. When Kant postulated that man was encumbered by "radical evil", Goethe—who really admired Kant very much—lost his temper; he wrote brutally that the elderly sage had "slobbered on his philosopher's cloak".

Goethe also veered from the main course of the Enlightenment in another way. His life—and his thought—were troubled by a great tension within himself which he never resolved, and never even brought into focus. He believed firmly in striving —in man's need to perfect himself through full and intense experience. But he also believed in a pitiless fate, a "demonic" force that all too often was stronger than man's reason. On one hand he preached action: "*Am Anfang war die Tat*"—in the beginning was the deed—runs a famous line in *Faust.* But meaningful activity was undercut by the need for resignation: "*Entsagen musst du, musst entsagen*"—Renounce you must, you must renounce. Some of this tension is simply the classical dichotomy which drives all men: emotion *versus* order. But some of it was not that happy or palatable; it was a dramatization not of discipline, but of impotence. Incapable of coping with the external world, Goethe turned his attention inwards, to an examination of himself. Thus in Germany the Enlightenment ended on an ambiguous note of introversion.

FAMOUS "PHILOSOPHES", *some of them key contributors to Diderot's Encyclopaedia, air their bold ideas at dinner. They are identified by numbers.*

# THE GREAT ENCYCLOPAEDIA

The intellectual crisis of the Enlightenment reached its climax in 1751 with the publication of the first volume of a great new encyclopaedia. This work, compiled by a society of liberal French thinkers, was far more than a mere collection of facts. It dared to preach the *philosophes'* radical credo that man could improve his lot if he replaced faith with reason as his guiding principle. It was, in sum, a threat to established authority in every field, from religion to government.

Inevitably the Encyclopaedia was suppressed. But its editor, Denis Diderot, though he had to go underground, did not waver in his determination to make useful knowledge widely available. He assured the brilliance of the work by securing articles from almost 200 distinguished experts and writers—a veritable Who's Who of the Enlightenment that included Voltaire, Rousseau and mathematician Jean d'Alembert. Diderot laboured on for 20 years, and in 1772, when his 28th and final volume was published, the Encyclopaedists were no longer in any personal danger. Their vast work had done much to conquer the age's intolerance, and it had laid a foundation for the era of revolutionary progress that lay ahead.

# AN AGE PRESERVED IN A GALLERY OF BRILLIANT PICTURES

A unique feature of Diderot's Encyclopaedia was its 11 volumes of superb engravings. Totalling some 3,000 pages of illustration, these books created a remarkable record of life in the mid-18th century; a sampling appears on the following pages. The picture books also had a tremendous impact on their time. Diderot's technical studies were useful to doctors and scientists. His industrial diagrams loosened the grip of monopolistic trade guilds by revealing their secret processes. Perhaps most important, Diderot raised the dignity of Europe's craftsman by presenting clear, step-by-step drawings that showed how to do everything from weaving lace to making rope.

Shown on these two pages are examples of the Encyclopaedia's pictorial coverage of warfare and weaponry. As a good editor, Diderot gave this subject all the space its importance deserved, though he personally rejected war as a legitimate means of furthering national interests. He observed regretfully that no courts existed to arbitrate between princes with conflicting ambitions; and therefore, he wrote, war or violence "is the only thing that can resolve them, and which ordinarily does".

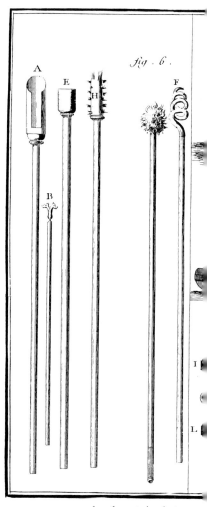

FIELD ARTILLERY *played a vital role in 18th-century warfare. The gun in Figure 2, a French-made bronze cannon that fired a 24-pound ball, was one of the many types used to breach fortifications. The gun's carriage is shown in profile in Figure 3 and from the top in Figure 4. The six staff-mounted implements on the left were used to load, fire and clean the piece. In battle, cannon like this were customarily wheeled into position by non-military personnel, and then fired by the professional gunners.*

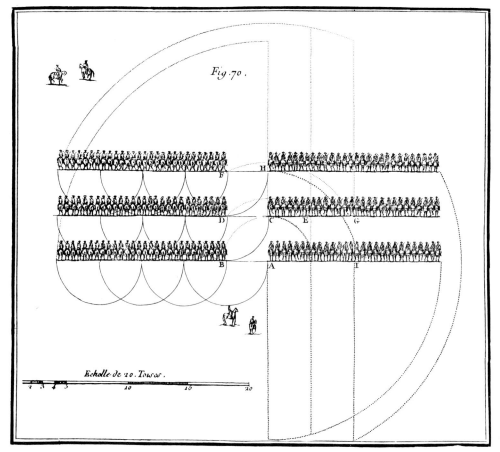

A CAVALRY MANŒUVRE *is illustrated in exquisite detail. Fully 168 horsemen, including four reviewing officers, are minutely portrayed against a precise scale (lower left). The dotted lines describe their movements. Pivoting clockwise, the left-hand ranks swung towards the top of the diagram, the right-hand ranks towards the bottom, thus forming three vertical columns.*

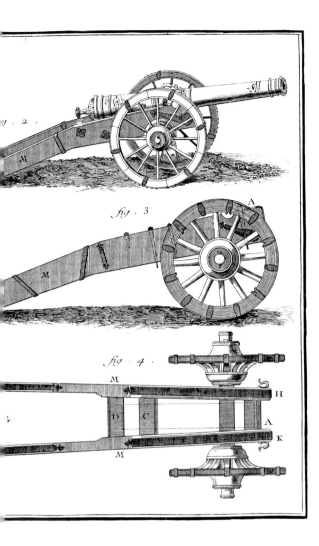

NAVAL TACTICS *in an age of great fleets called for complicated manœuvres and innumerable signals. The warship in Figure 5 hangs a lantern on its mainmast and fires one cannon to signal that it is preparing to weather a storm. In Figure 6 a ship signals its intention to pursue a straight course by flying a white pennant on the mainmast and firing two cannon. Figure 12 shows, with dotted lines, how a cluster of men-of-war, flying white ensigns, manœuvres into a single file. From this standard battle formation, each ship could rake the enemy with broadsides in passing.*

INFANTRY ARMS *were developed in great variety for Europe's large standing armies. A French-made flintlock, seen over-all in Figure 1 below, is shown broken down into its major assemblages. The firing mechanism is shown in the cocked position in Figure 2; further details of this assemblage include two views (Figures 4 and 5) of the flint-bearing hammer. When the trigger was pulled, the flint struck a protruding leaf of grooved steel (Figure 3). The resultant spark ignited the weapon's powder charge and fired the crude lead musket ball—with notoriously inaccurate results.*

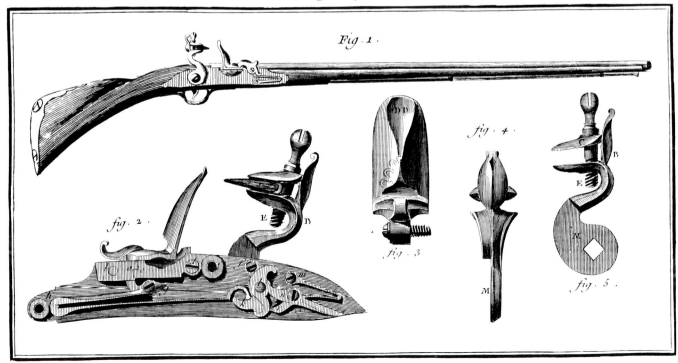

# An illustrated catalogue of surgical practices

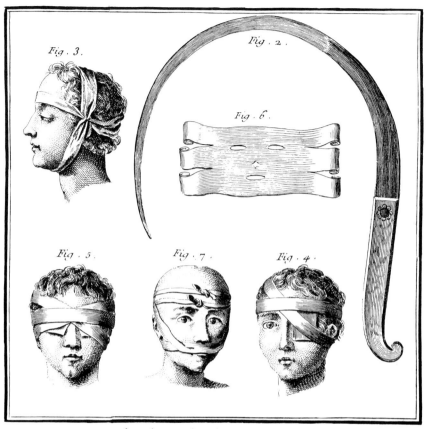

MEDICAL ILLUSTRATIONS *from the Encyclopaedia depict five types of facial bandages and a sickle-shaped scalpel known as a bistoury. The use of such surgical instruments and the practice of medicine were unrelated professions in the 18th century. Surgeons had little schooling and were not even considered doctors. They usually started their careers as barbers.*

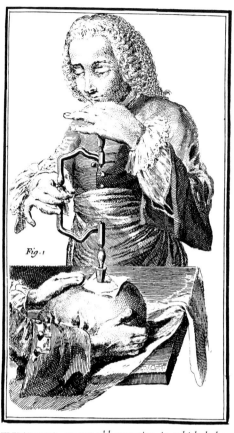

TREPANNING, *an age-old operation in which holes are bored in the cranium to relieve pressure on the brain, was practised with an adjustable steel drill that resembled a carpenter's brace and bit.*

OPERATING TOOLS *of the 18th century bear a marked resemblance to their refined modern descendants. The small bone-cutter (Figure 3), the mallet for tapping bone fragments into place (Figure 6), the "crow's beak" clamp (Figure 7) and the bone saw (Figure 1) are, with modifications, in use to-day. Cutting pincers (Figure 2), scissors for splinters (Figure 4), and forceps for removing bullets (Figure 5) have no exact modern counterparts.*

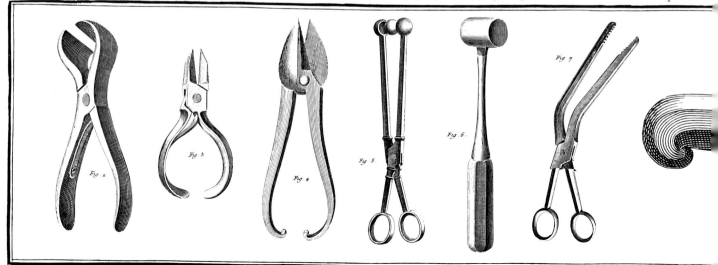

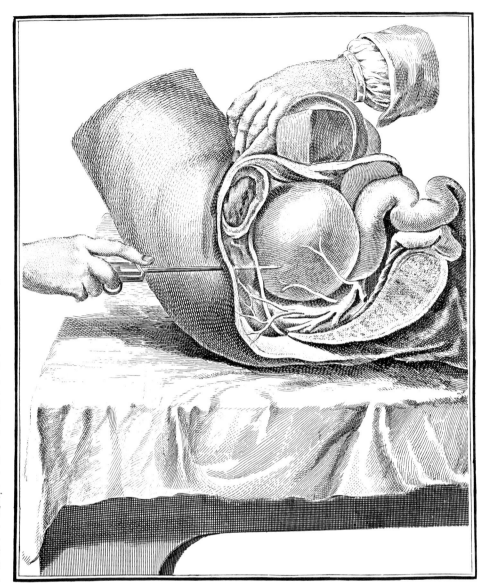

MAJOR SURGERY *was a risky business in an age that had no anaesthetics or antiseptics, and the Encyclopaedia warned its readers to submit to such operations only as a last resort. The engraving on the right was presented to suggest a possible surgical approach to the problem of a painful stone lodged in the bladder: a long, tubular instrument might be inserted into the bladder to drain off urine; then, through the same incision, thin pincers could probe for and remove the stone. Medical conditions slowly reflected the age's growing reliance on scientific methods. The dangerous practice of blood-letting and the excessive use of drugs met with stronger opposition. A system of clinical observation was begun; careful studies of symptoms and case histories confirmed the Encyclopaedia's view that "Experience is the source of substantial principles; and any knowledge that is not purified by thoughtful application can be nothing more than a false glimmer".*

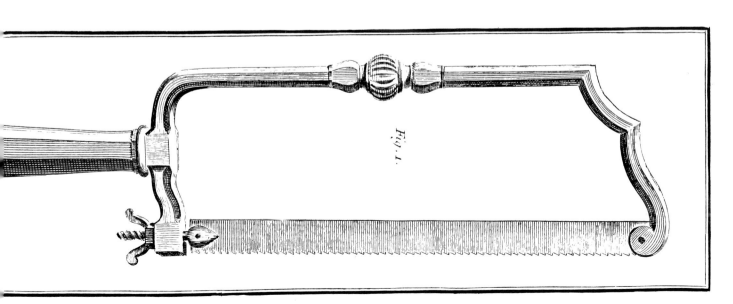

*Fig. 1.*

# Men at work: trades and crafts

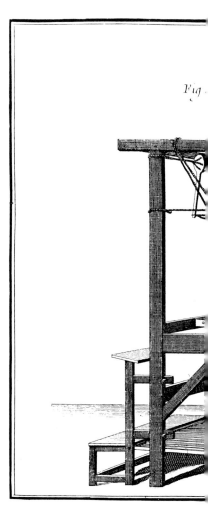

ROPE-MAKING *required teamwork (below). Four workmen (left) pay out four strands; two men (right) turn a crank that twists the strands into one cable around a "wick" watched by the master rope-maker. This rope is seen in cross-section in Figure 7 with other cables.*

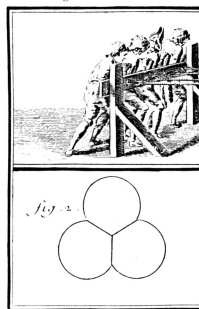

A MODEL MINE, *shown in cross-section, emphasized ideal standards rather than the grim reality of mining operations in the 18th century. The miners descended to work by ladder. The ore, which they transported to the three shafts by wheelbarrow (Figure 5), was hauled to the surface by hand-cranked winches (Figures 3 and 4) and by a large* windlass *(Figure 1) housed in a wood roundabout and turned by horses. Despite the shoring shown in the bottom gallery (Figure 7), cave-ins were common, as were occupational diseases such as silicosis. Diderot laid the blame for these bad conditions —and for almost everything else that went wrong in France—on superstition and the idle nobility.*

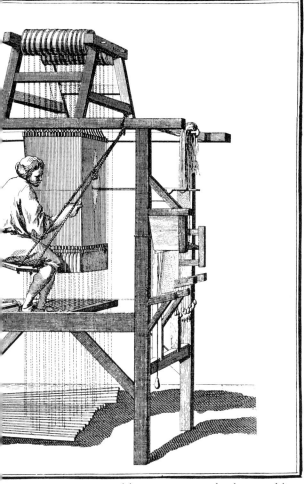

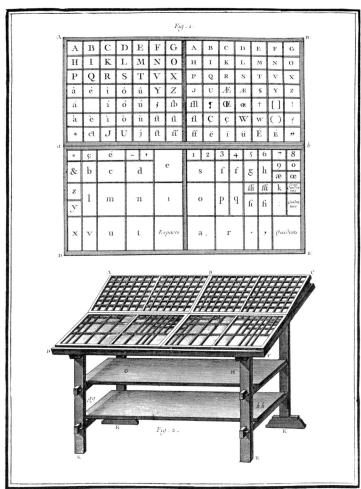

A GIANT LOOM *is used by a weaver to make the most delicate fabrics, such as lace and fancy ribbon. Weavers and other artisans jealously concealed their special formulas and methods, but Diderot, who learned his respect for the craftsman while watching his father work as a master cutler, published such detailed studies of the crafts that he revealed many trade secrets.*

THE PRINTER'S TRADE *was represented by an angled fount case (Figure 2), used to store hand-set type. As Figure 1 shows, each of the case's 152 compartments held a different letter or symbol; the upper section held capital letters and the flat section held small letters—hence the modern typographic terms "upper case" and "lower case". Printing was then highly advanced; the Encyclopaedia itself was a superb product of fine typography and accurate presswork.*

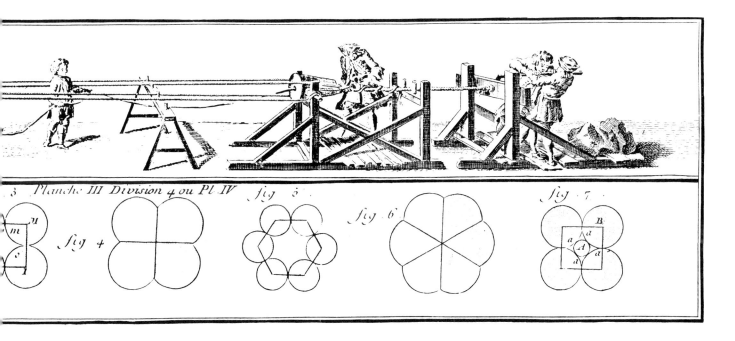

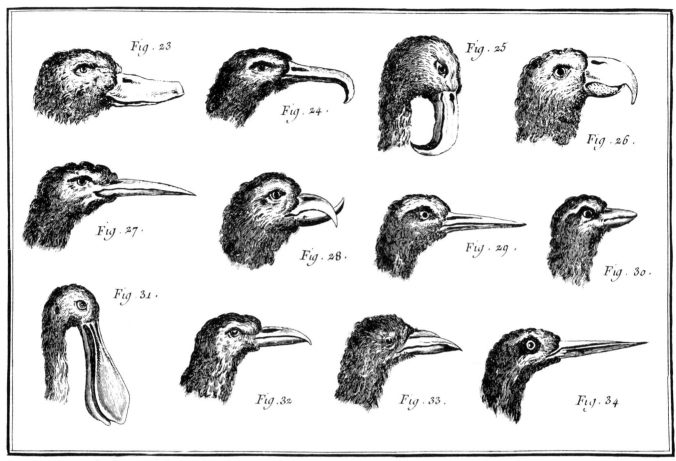

EXOTIC BIRDS *caught the eye of the encyclopaedists, who classified the birds' bills according to an easy system of recognition. Thus the bill in Figure 25 was labelled a "scythe-shaped beak", the one in Figure 29 an "awl-shaped" beak and the one in Figure 31 a "spatula beak". Yet un-like many men of the Enlightenment, Diderot and his colleagues were not interested in simply classifying things by names. They hoped that as a result of their graphic presentation, readers would examine and compare the differences between members of a given animal family.*

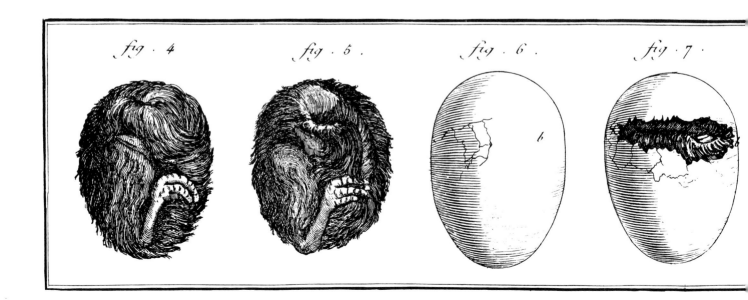

Fig. 3

Fig. 5

Fig. 4

Fig. 1

REPTILIAN CURIOSITIES *of the day are noted in the drawings on the left which, like a number of the Encyclopaedia's illustrations, were lifted from other contemporary sources. The writhing snake is a female viper found in France, depicted in the act of giving birth. With it are two details, one of the viper's head, showing its venomous fangs and tongue, the other its birth sac, which shelters the young snake until birth. Lurking beneath the viper is a small and less noxious Egyptian lizard called a skink, which the encyclopaedists thought worth portraying because of an allegedly antitoxic substance that its glands secrete.*

A HATCHING CHICK *in its birth struggles, trying to separate itself from its egg, is analysed in the sequence of drawings below. In Figures 4 and 5 the egg-shell is removed to show the chick as a fully formed and feathered youngster ready to peck its way to freedom. In Figure 6 the shell has begun to crack at the correct point, but in Figure 7 an accident occurs: the egg and its lining, or membrane, rupture, exposing the chick to the air prematurely. The proper process (and therefore the one admired by the "philosophes") is sketched in Figures 8 and 9: having created a perfect lid, the chick has only to lift the top and emerge. The last two sketches show, with encyclopaedic thoroughness, the condition of the shell and membrane after the chick has waddled away.*

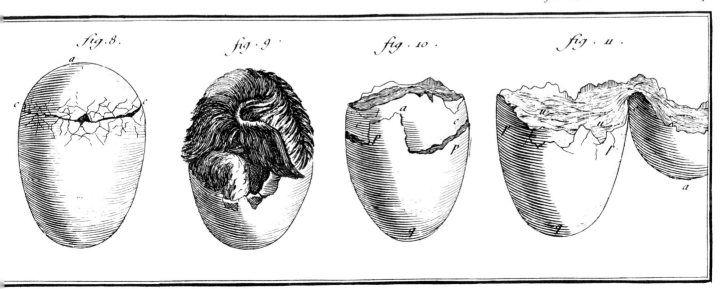

fig. 8.

fig. 9.

fig. 10.

fig. 11.

# Instructive pictures of sports and games

THE ART OF FENCING could be either a harmless sport or a deadly contest. The Encyclopaedia showed the fencer's blunt-tipped foil (Figure 1) and gear—shoes, gloves, face mask and body covering. When the sportsman's honour was at stake he took up an unblunted sword (Figure 2).

Armed with such weapons, the duellists in Figure 31 demonstrate a high thrust (left) that exposes the body and, from the right, a fatal thrust driven into the opening. The moral, Diderot told his readers, was "never to plan a thrust without being able to return promptly to a parry".

COURT TENNIS, a net game that long pre-dated today's lawn tennis, had its heyday in the 17th century. Solid-wood paddles (Figures 6 and 7) were precursors of the racket (Figure 5), whose open face was crisscrossed with string woven through the frame (seen in profile in Figure

4) and anchored with an intricate knot (Figure 12). The ball was made of a cloth core wrapped in string (Figures 8, 9 and 10), then covered with fabric (Figure 11). An engraving of two doubles teams playing court tennis shows the elaborate and costly court that the game required.

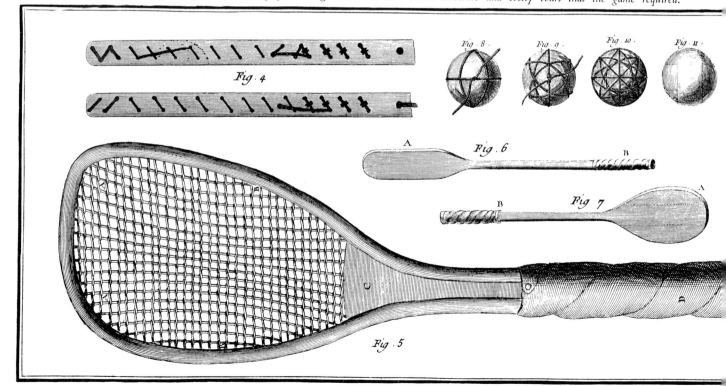

EQUESTRIAN COMPETITION, *like most sports of the age, was primarily a pastime for wealthy noblemen. It took a well-filled purse to buy and train a stylish horse such as the one on the right, shown executing a manœuvre described exactly by its name, "the rump against the wall". To make the exercise unmistakably clear, an accompanying diagram shows the steed's slightly angled stance and its cross-over footwork as it moves along sideways. The outer dotted line traces the path of the horse's haunches; its shoulders follow the inner dotted line. The rider, after showing how well his mount moves to its right (left wall), goes to the facing wall and puts the beast through its paces moving to the left. They end up at the centre.*

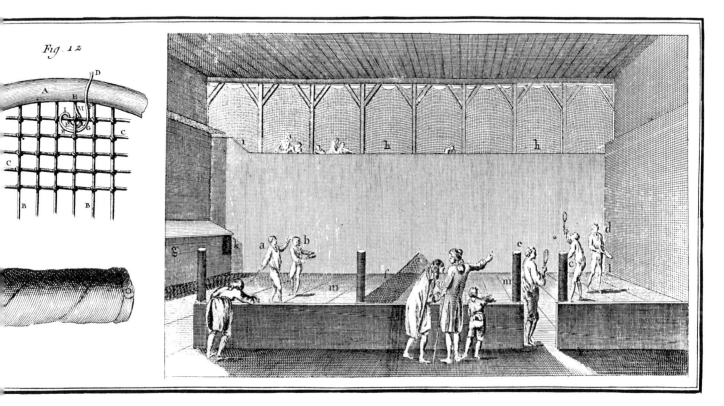

# Muscle, wind and water to turn the wheels of industry

MANPOWER *was the prime mover of industry at the start of the 18th century. Among the many machines operated by muscle was the elaborate press shown in the engraving on the right. A workman walks on the revolving steps of a treadmill, driving pulleys which lower the press's wooden lid. Such a contraption might be used to compress bulky cotton into a manageable bale. Muscle power, whether supplied by man or animals, had severe limitations; industry drew more and more of its power from sources in nature— not only the rivers but also fire, newly used to vaporize water and thus to run machines by steam. James Watt's steam engine, patented in set the stage for the Industrial Revolution.*

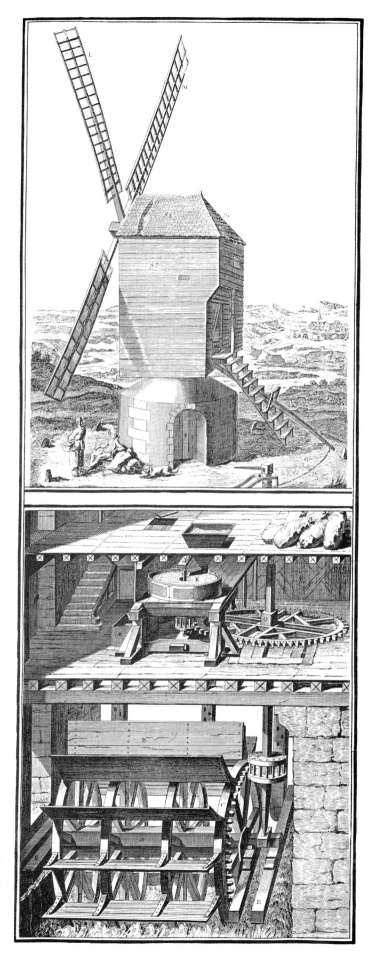

HORSEPOWER *helped to run the brass foundry shown here. The horse turns grinding wheels that crush crude zinc. The workman in Figure 6 cranks a barrel that mixes the zinc with the copper needed to make brass alloy. In Figure 11, five men use an ungainly apparatus to scrape a mould for molten brass. The finished sheets of brass are cut by huge scissors whose jaws are closed by three men pushing a lever (Figure 12). Because these processes needed frequent attention, the workmen had to sleep and eat in the foundry.*

WIND AND WATER *served to mill grain into flour in the 18th century as they had for centuries. The windmill shown in the top picture was mounted on a post or pivot; the whole structure rotated to face into the wind. Below, the more reliable water-wheel is shown driving gears and shafts that turned the wheels that milled the grain. At about mid-century, water-wheels were also being put to modern industrial use, and their prior function fathered misnomers that persist to this day, such as "steel mill" and "cotton mill".*

# 8

# "A NEW AGE BEGINS"

The Age of Enlightenment was an age of ferment, but most of that ferment was expressed in words rather than action. Not until the close of the 18th century did the arguments erupt into revolution and war. Although the two great empires of England and France fought each other intermittently all through the century, their encounters were contained military actions, fought much like chess games over fixed terrains, for the purpose of imperial expansion. Compared with the wars of the preceding century, which had devastated much of central Europe, they seemed relatively mild. In fact, to men of the 18th century, their age seemed one of peace. The spreading criticism of Christianity, the accelerating pace of the Industrial Revolution, the steady increase in population—all these things might point to change, even drastic change. But they gave no hint—at least to men of the time—of the series of events, particularly the French Revolution and its aftermath, which would disrupt the whole Western world.

Nevertheless, there were ominous rumblings. Beginning in the 1760's, country after country was afflicted with political unrest. In little States like Geneva and large States like England, radical politicians and radical associations were challenging the established order. Everywhere their basic demands were the same: the right to participate in politics, the right to vote, the right to greater freedom of expression. And although demands of this nature were seldom voiced in the authoritarian States of central and eastern Europe—in Prussia, Russia and Habsburg Austria—even here there was change. New ideas might not penetrate the wall of political censorship, but sometimes they were introduced, in carefully controlled ways, from above.

Prussia, under Frederick the Great, reduced the severity of the punishment for certain crimes—or at least Frederick thought he had done so. The crime of infanticide, for example, was now punished by beheading instead of by drowning in a leather sack (which for added penance the accused had often been forced to stitch up himself). Frederick also invited *philosophes* to his court and preached religious tolerance. In Russia, the Empress Catherine, also fancying herself enlightened, caused a commission to be elected for the

THE PASSING OF ELEGANCE *is suggested in this painting made by Goya in 1778. Prominent in the foreground are some peasant women haggling over pottery. More subdued in emphasis is the figure of the noblewoman flashing by in her carriage, already an anachronism in a world ripe for revolution.*

purpose of examining and modernizing Russia's laws. The commission consulted endlessly, but fruitlessly, guided by Catherine's instructions, which were based on her reading of Montesquieu's *Spirit of the Laws*. If the commission's activities came to nothing, that was Catherine's doing too, for she refused to act on most of the matters raised in its deliberations.

Meanwhile, in Austria, Maria Theresa modernized the administration of her State and bettered the lot of the Austrian peasant by lightening his conditions of servitude, although her motives were not wholly altruistic—she wanted to consolidate her power. Her son Joseph, who followed her on the throne and was tremendously keen on enlightenment, freed serfs from their long bondage to the land, lifted some of the sanctions against Protestants and Jews in Roman Catholic Austria, and removed some of the shackles from the press.

Europe did not think it was heading towards open revolt. Quite the contrary, it thought that by introducing new ideas it would alleviate the conditions that spawned revolt. And then, in 1775, came the American Revolution.

For a decade or more, Europe had been watching developments in the British colonies in America with considerable interest. There had been constant controversy with the mother country since the 1760's, and as the years went by, the controversy deepened. But the full significance of these events —and their meaning for the Enlightenment—did not become clear until the Revolution itself. The struggle seemed largely internal, between tough-minded, politically mature colonists and an equally determined government back home. But between the shot heard round the world on the 19th April 1775 and the surrender at Yorktown on the 19th October 1781, the American Revolution took on a new light.

"We wished the Americans all success," Goethe later recalled in his autobiography, ". . . the names of Franklin and Washington began to shine and sparkle in the firmament of politics and war." The revolution in America made sense of the ferment in Europe. Here were free men resisting, first by arguments and then by arms, what enthusiastically pro-American Europeans called "tyranny". It was a great lesson—a lesson to ponder and perhaps to imitate. To fond European observers, the American settlers had long appeared admirable men, true men of the Enlightenment—cultivated yet simple in their tastes, rational yet passionately concerned about equality, peaceful yet ready to go to war for their freedom. Now, by wresting independence from a formidable imperial power, the colonists had proved that the Enlightenment ideas worked. They had been tested in the hardest laboratory of all, the laboratory to which the Enlightenment liked to submit all its ideas: experience.

The triumph of Enlightenment ideas in America appeared all the more dazzling because in Europe it looked as though those ideas might fail. True, they had made influential converts everywhere: men of God talked about reasonable Christianity, pious rulers expelled Jesuits from their realms, and the humanitarian ideas of men like Voltaire spread throughout Europe. But at the same time, the kinds of political and legislative reforms suggested by these ideas failed to materialize. In spite of the *philosophes* and their pamphlets, and the politicians and their speeches, very little seemed to happen.

In France, a time of great test came after 1774, when Louis XV died. Louis's reign had not been very productive of reform, although he had tried. Urged on by ministers, he had sought to tax the clergy and impose controls on the French nobility. But he had failed. When Louis died, reform in France seemed as far away as it had when he had come to the throne, a five-year-old boy, 59 years before. His successor, however, the youthful Louis

XVI, showed promise of making reform a reality.

Among the new Louis' first appointments was the *philosophe* Anne Robert Jacques Turgot, whom Louis made minister of Marine and then, one month later, Controller-General of Finance. Turgot was a *philosophe*'s *philosophe*. A brilliant intellectual who had gained fame in his early twenties with a dissertation, "On the Historical Progress of the Human Mind", he had then turned to public service and accumulated a distinguished record. Turgot was a practical politician, versed in the ways of the world, not just a Utopian dreamer.

Once in power, Turgot developed a programme of economic reform that confirmed the other *philosophes*' faith in him, but aroused the opposition of vested interests. Looking to liberate trade within France, he proposed that internal tariffs and guild regulations be abolished (the first restricted the circulation of grain; the second, the free pursuit of trades or professions). To make things worse, he also advocated tax revisions that would have spread the tax burden equally through all levels of society, and he proposed that Protestants be granted full civil rights.

Turgot did not last long. Appointed in August 1774, he was summarily dismissed in May 1776. "It is not my purpose to mingle the orders of society", announced the appalled Louis. The dismissal left the *philosophes* dismayed. Turgot had been something of a test case for them. For half a century they had been trying and failing to bring about reforms, and time was getting short. If an experienced and trustworthy public servant like Turgot could not survive the opposition of the selfish reactionary forces within the government, how could any reform ever succeed?

"The dismissal of this great man", wrote Voltaire, "crushes me. . . . Since that fatal day, I have not followed anything, I have not asked anyone for anything, and I am waiting patiently for someone

to cut our throats." That was how many other Frenchmen saw it too, and they had a right to be gloomy. In the 1770's and 1780's evidence accumulated that the French State faced political and economic bankruptcy. It was borrowing huge sums from European bankers and falsifying records to hide the true state of its finances. In addition, high living among the clergy, scandals touching the personal life of Queen Marie Antoinette (she was accused of offering her favours to a cardinal in exchange for a diamond necklace), and a series of bad harvests in the strategic French wine industry all contributed to an atmosphere of disquietude.

Louis tried to make repairs. In 1787 he called together a council of notables to deal with the State's financial crisis. Then in 1789, after this measure had failed, he convened the Estates-General, a national assembly representing the three traditional divisions in French society—the clergy, the nobility, and the common people.

Controversy sprang up immediately over how the assembly should conduct its business—it had not met for 175 years, and its powers had never been clearly defined. The aristocracy and the clergy, seeking to preserve their traditional privileges, wanted each Estate to vote as a unit. This would have left control of the assembly with the upper classes. The common people, comprising the Third Estate, wanted each man to vote as an individual. Since their representation in the assembly had recently been enlarged to 50 per cent of the total membership, and they reckoned on the support of liberals in the other two Estates, this would have given them numerical control.

Popular agitation over this issue grew intense, and revolutionary sentiments spread. When the King would not honour the Third Estate's demands, the commoners broke away from the Estates-General to form their own National Assembly. The rest is history.

On the 14th July 1789, an enraged Parisian crowd stormed the Bastille: the Crown could no longer keep order; from then on, the French populace had to be counted as a political force. By the end of August of the same year most of the French aristocracy's traditional feudal privileges had been wiped out and a bold "Declaration of the Rights of Man and of the Citizen" had passed into law.

The Declaration codified most of the demands of the Enlightenment: it declared that the natural rights of man—"liberty, property, security and resistance to oppression"—were sacred and inalienable; it established men's right to express their opinions freely; it radically revised French criminal law by forbidding arbitrary arrest and protecting the rights of the accused. It also declared that France was not the private property of its monarchs, but a sovereign nation owned by its people. The language of the Declaration is rather abstract, as such documents tend to be, but its individual points were specifically related to the historical experiences of the French people. In it, the ideals of the Enlightenment and the practicalities of politics meet and merge.

But even in 1789 it was clear to far-sighted men that, for all its rightness, the Declaration was not likely to upset the old order so easily. Before it could truly alter French society, it would have to survive the manipulations of politicians, the demands of an aroused but politically ill-trained citizenry, and the determined resistance of groups with a vested interest in the existing government. It seemed most unlikely that a nobility which had held its privileges for many centuries would surrender those privileges without a struggle. It seemed equally unlikely that the French Crown, which had spent centuries fighting for absolute rule, would consent to limiting its power to constitutional monarchy. And it seemed unlikely that a privileged clergy, exempt from taxation, would agree to become no more than a body of paid clerks, controlled by the public.

Finally, it seemed unlikely that the rest of monarchial Europe would stand idly by and watch the triumph of ideas so inimical to their own interests—especially when, in their own countries, there were radicals, liberals and anticlericals who looked upon the French Revolution as a prelude to their own.

And so the Age of Enlightenment became the Age of Revolution and War. In the brief 10 years before the century ended, France formed a republic, executed a king, established an effective if faction-ridden revolutionary régime, and passed from that through a period of confusion that ended with a *coup d'état* and Napoleon's accession to power in 1799. Through it all, the French nation continually fought the rest of Europe.

When the new century dawned, some gains had been scuttled and others preserved. But two things were clear: the old Europe was dead, and the Enlightenment, however compromised, had survived. One observer foresaw both conclusions when the Revolution was still young. In the late summer of 1792 the German poet Goethe was attached to a contingent of soldiers from Weimar, fighting with a combined Prussian-Austrian army then invading France. Goethe, with his Olympian detachment, was neither for nor against the revolutionary cause. He fully expected to witness the occupation of Paris and the Revolution's defeat. Instead it happened otherwise. On the 20th September the French defeated the allied German armies at Valmy, and the Revolution triumphed. After the battle, seated in a circle with his silent and dejected companions, Goethe prophetically summed up for them the meaning of the day's events.

"Here and today", said Goethe, "begins a new age in the history of the world. Some day you will all be able to say—I was present at its birth."

A PORCELAIN FANTASY *lining the walls of an Italian salon is made of more than 3,000 separate pieces.*

# TWILIGHT OF THE ARTISAN

In its insatiable quest for beauty in every aspect of life, 18th-century Europe, led by France, demanded and received extraordinary accomplishments from its craftsmen. Hand-workers transformed the most ordinary appurtenances—walls, furniture, cutlery and table-ware—into true works of art and, in the process, forged themselves into consummate artists. Towards the end of the century, when hints of the Industrial Revolution began to appear, all ranks of artisans seem, in retrospect, to have shared one compulsion: to show the world the extravagance of their skill before technology made it superfluous. The evidence can be seen in the Neapolitan porcelain room above, and on the pages that follow.

# HIGH SKILL IN WOODWORK

Men who made fine furniture were skilled and temperamental specialists. A designer planned a chair, table or chest to follow the decorative motif of the room in which it would stand. A *menuisier*, or carpenter, planed and joined oak or fir to form the basic structure, then stepped back while a sculptor carved it into intricate relief. Still another specialist was available to gild or paint, when required.

The *menuisier* also prepared the wood's surface for the *ébéniste*, who was master of veneers and marquetry. For veneering, such artists could hand-saw pieces of ebony, rosewood or the newly popular mahogany into sheets barely two millimetres thick, which were then applied to the piece with glue and a warm iron. In marquetry, sheets of natural, painted or stained woods were further cut into jigsaw pieces and applied in similar manner to form decorative panels such as the Chinese scene on the left. In another age, such art would be framed and hung on a wall. In 18th-century Europe, it was applied to a desk as exquisite as the ladies and gentlemen who employed it to write their frivolous notes.

FRENCH TECHNIQUES IN WOOD, *shown in the delicately carved oak panel of an armoire (far left) and an elegantly gilded chair leg (centre), also spread beyond France: the inlaid marquetry was made by the German "ébéniste" David Röntgen as a decorative panel for a roll-top desk.*

# A MAGNITUDE IN MINIATURE

THE CHOISEUL SNUFF-BOX, *only 3⅛ by 2⅜ by 1⁷⁄₁₆ inches, details the interiors of a nobleman's Paris house. On the box's lid is the scene below.*

Etienne-François de Choiseul-Stainville, duc de Choiseul et d'Amboise, was not a modest man. Secure in his post as Louis XV's first minister—a position maintained both by diligence and by Madame de Pompadour's gratitude for a discreet favour—he elected to have himself, his home and his art collection portrayed as the motif of a tiny snuff-box. He commissioned six miniature scenes from Henri-Désiré van Blarenberghe to be set under crystal in a framework by the Parisian goldsmith Louis Roucel. While Roucel's work could stand alone as art, the marvel of the Choiseul box is its painted panels, such perfect examples of the miniaturist's art that even the paintings within the paintings remain precise and clear when magnified many times.

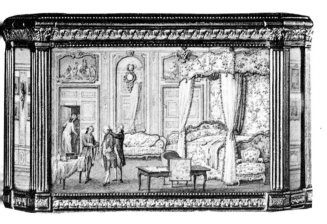

A FAMOUS ART COLLECTION *decorated Choiseul's intimate dressing room (above), as well as the Octagon Room (below), which had a glass dome specially designed to light his favourite paintings. In miniature, none of these paintings is more than half an inch across, yet most are identifiable, including four Rembrandts on the left wall of the reception room (right centre). In the study (right bottom), paintings share honours with a large, ornate writing desk and matching filing cabinet at which the duke and his secretaries work. As first minister, Choiseul's dedication to duty runs as a theme through the panels, but only one shows him outside his home. In this one (right top), he looks at plans in the Grande Galerie of the Louvre shortly before the removal of its relief maps and model fortifications began transforming the great palace into today's museum.*

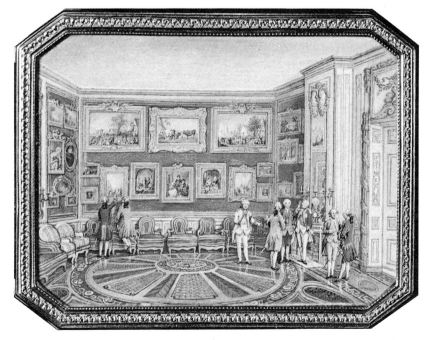

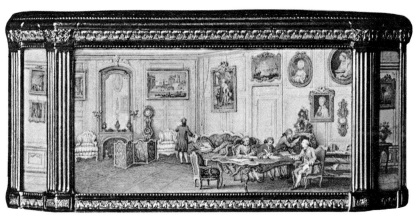

# THE DELIGHTS OF PORCELAIN

The German *arcanist* had no opposite number in any other field of decorative art: he was originally any deserter from Meissen who spread the highly guarded secret (in Latin, *arcanum*) of making hard-paste porcelain. Unlike silver, wood or tapestry, porcelain was an unfamiliar material in the West until the China trade brought it to Europe along with tea and silk. When pottery craftsmen saw this white, hard, translucent and resonant ceramic ware, they were stunned; beside it their own work seemed coarse and crude. Still, they might never have re-produced the porcelain if Augustus the Strong of Saxony and Poland had not been such an obsessive collector that he virtually forced Johann Friedrich Böttger to discover the Chinese formula.

Böttger, an alchemist by profession, analysed various kinds of clay and was finally able to duplicate the Chinese recipe. With the secret in hand, Augustus promptly built a factory at Meissen in 1710 to manufacture the first true European porcelain. From there, roving *arcanists* helped to spread the technique through Germany, France, Italy and Russia.

A MERCHANT AT HIS DESK *(right) was first copied in clay from an original Meissen figurine. A worker cut the model into pieces and made separate moulds of the upper body, chair, desk and other sections. The moulds were filled with liquid porcelain mix, removed when it had partly dried, and the pieces assembled before painting and firing.*

A FRIGHTENED GIRL, *delicately shying from a snake, was made of a blend of white kaolin clay and petuntse, a powdered rock. These raw materials were shaped, fired and painted, then glazed and fired once more at 1,450° C. Porcelain made by this toughening process does not fade: its colours are the truest record of the 18th-century palette.*

FINE TEXTURE, *shown here in a close-up of a pair of birds—seen also on the far right in the room below—was woven at 22 to 24 strands to an inch.*

RICH DETAILING *was enhanced by leaving dark, open slits where varying shades of colour meet. French tapestry weavers used wool and silk yarns in some 10,000 different hues.*

AN ALL-TAPESTRY ROOM, *commissioned by the sixth Earl of Coventry for his house at Croome Court, displays Gobelins work, including "paintings", on furniture and walls.*

# A TRIUMPH OF TAPESTRY

Behind the ornamental hand-work that decorated 18th-century Europe rode a phalanx of hard-working, harried and inventive men beset by familiar problems. One of them was Jacques-Germain Soufflot, director of Louis XV's royal tapestry manufactory of Gobelins. Soufflot was bedevilled by weavers who occasionally caroused at the gatekeeper's house and engaged in sword-play at work. But his greatest problem was money. The king, his primary customer, neglected to pay his bills, and the Gobelins looms could not produce work rapidly and cheaply enough to supply a clientele beyond the Court. High vertical looms, on which the best tapestry was woven, required too much manual labour; low horizontal looms, with foot pedals that speeded the shuttle, produced slightly inferior work, mainly because the tapestry faced the floor. Soufflot, however, invented a low loom that allowed its user to see his work from the front and correct it to high-loom perfection. Thus he was able to solicit Gobelins commissions from private individuals, even foreigners, who unlike the king would pay in cash on time.

# THE DISCIPLINES OF FINE METAL

Eighteenth-century gold- and silversmiths practised their sophisticated trade according to the rules of guilds as closed and meticulous as those of the Middle Ages. Each man served an eight-year apprenticeship to a master smith and two or three years more as a journeyman before he was permitted to stand for examination by the stern guild wardens. Only after he had met their standards of knowledge, skill and integrity—and submitted an acceptable "master piece"—could he open his shop.

AN ELEGANT BOX, *called a "nécessaire" (left), was used to hold such necessities as watches, needles, perfumes, powders and sealing-wax. These miniature chests were equipped with finely wrought fittings and were finished in gold, agate and precious stones.*

A NOBLE EGG-CUP *(right) intended for everyday use, testifies to the skill of the 18th-century silversmith: his patrons commanded elegance even in utilitarian objects 3 ⅝ inches high.*

A DELICATE CAMEO *of a woman's head is part of the border of a silver glove tray. It was only in the 18th century that gold and silver objects came into everyday secular use.*

# A BRAVURA
# OF GLASS

Among the arts to which craftsmen gave
their hearts and the wit of their hands was
Venetian glass. The function of this five-
by eight-foot glass garden was, simply, to
make a banquet table superb. The custom
of dining at a huge table began in the 18th
century; inevitably fashion required that
a masterpiece decorate the centre.

The small, movable parts of this glass
centrepiece were grouped to imitate the
fountains, ponds, arches and flowers of the
period's elaborate gardens. Although the
many decorative urns are solid milk glass,
which was pinched into shape while glowing hot, most of the work is hollow clear
glass, blown from molten bulbs at the end
of masters' pipes. The master and two or
three assistants who made this *trionfo da
tavola* ("table triumph") were so skilful that
they could spin glass water jets from a
fountain or perch a glass butterfly on a
flower petal. Such bravura craftsmanship
made the Enlightenment one of the greatest ages of hand-work the world has known.

# APPENDIX

## GREAT AGES OF WESTERN CIVILISATION

The chart on the right is designed to show the duration of the Age of Enlightenment, the subject of this volume, and to relate it to the other cultures of the Western world that are considered in one major group of volumes in this series. This chart will enable the reader to relate the great ages of Western civilization to important cultures in other parts of the world, some of which are the subjects of other volumes in the series.

On the next two pages is a chronological table of important events which took place during the era covered by this book.

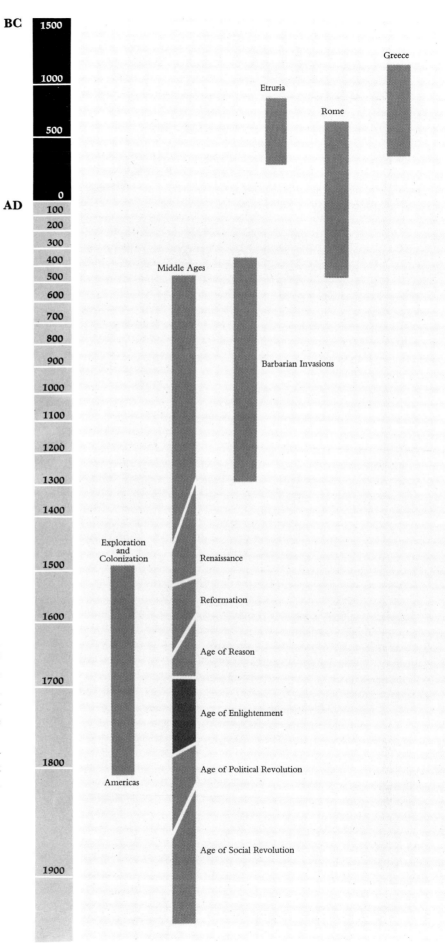

BC

1500

1000

500

0

AD

100
200
300
400
500
600
700
800
900
1000
1100
1200
1300
1400
1500
1600
1700
1800
1900

Greece

Etruria

Rome

Middle Ages

Barbarian Invasions

Exploration and Colonization

Renaissance

Reformation

Age of Reason

Age of Enlightenment

Age of Political Revolution

Americas

Age of Social Revolution

# CHRONOLOGY: A history of significant events during the Age of Enlightenment

## Politics and Society

**1685** Louis XIV revokes the Edict of Nantes, bringing persecution and emigration of the Huguenots

**1688–1689** Glorious Revolution establishes the supremacy of Parliament in England, deposes James II, puts Protestant William and Mary on the throne

**1689** Peter the Great takes full power as Tsar of Russia

**1697** Treaty of Ryswick ends the War of the Augsburg League

**1701** Act of Settlement ensures Protestant succession to the throne; reign of Queen Anne follows; Grand Alliance wages War of the Spanish Succession against Louis XIV

**1704** French are defeated at Blenheim by the Duke of Marlborough

**1705** Thomas Newcomen constructs an improved steam pump

**1709** Marlborough and Prince Eugene of Savoy defeat Villars at Malplaquet; the convent of Port-Royal is closed by Louis XIV in a move against the Jansenists

**1713** Peace of Utrecht ends French predominance in Europe

**1714** Protestant George I of House of Hanover succeeds Queen Anne

**1715** Louis XV begins reign with Philip, Duke of Orléans, as Regent

**1720** John Law's financial "system" and the Mississippi scheme bring speculation and financial collapse in France; South Sea bubble bursts in England

**1721** Whig Robert Walpole begins his 21-year tenure as England's principal Minister of State

**1723** The Regent dies and young Louis XV becomes full ruler of France

**1726** Fleury becomes Louis's chief adviser and principal minister for 17 years

**1727** George II is crowned King of England

**1733** John Kay patents the flying shuttle, initiating modern mechanical weaving

**1735** Two-year War of the Polish Succession ends with the Treaty of Vienna

**1739** England and Spain fight the War of Jenkins' Ear over New World trade

**1740** Frederick the Great assumes the throne in Prussia; Maria Theresa becomes head of the Habsburg empire; Prussia and France, allied against Austria and England, begin the War of the Austrian Succession

**1744** England and France fight King George's War in Nova Scotia and India

**1745** Madame de Pompadour becomes Louis XV's mistress

## A.D.

1690

1700

1710

1720

1730

1740

## Thought and Culture

**1685** Bach is born in Eisenach; Handel is born in Halle

**1687** Newton's *Principia Mathematica* is published

**1690** Locke's *Second Treatise of Civil Government* appears, is used in defence of England's Glorious Revolution

**1694** François Marie Arouet (Voltaire) is born in Paris

**1696** English deist John Toland publishes *Christianity Not Mysterious*

**1697** Pierre Bayle issues his *Critical and Philosophical Dictionary*, a major source for 18th-century philosophers

**1700** Gottfried Leibnitz becomes first president of the Berlin Society of Sciences

**1704** Newton, President of the Royal Society of London, publishes *Opticks*; Daniel Defoe starts the *Review*

**1709** *The Tatler* begins publication under editor Richard Steele

**1710** Handel becomes musical director to the Elector of Hanover, later George I of England

**1711** *The Spectator*, written by Joseph Addison and Richard Steele, starts daily publication

**1714** Alexander Pope's *The Rape of the Lock* ridicules fashionable society

**1717** Benjamin Hoadly, Bishop of Bangor, denies in sermon that Church has worldly power

**1718** Arouet assumes the name Voltaire, publishes his first tragedy, *Oedipus*

**1719** Daniel Defoe's *Robinson Crusoe* appears

**1721** Montesquieu's *Persian Letters*, satirizing French institutions, brings its author fame

**1723** Bach becomes music director in Leipzig, remains until death in 1750

**1726** Jonathan Swift completes his masterpiece, *Gulliver's Travels*

**1728** First performance is given of *The Beggar's Opera* by playwright John Gay

**1731** Prévost's romantic novel *Manon Lescaut* appears

**1733** Voltaire completes his *Philosophical Letters on the English*

**1735** William Hogarth's *The Rake's Progress* and Carl Linnaeus's *System of Nature* are published

**1736** Joseph Butler writes *The Analogy of Religion* refuting deism

**1739** Methodist John Wesley starts his preaching mission; David Hume writes *Treatise of Human Nature*

**1740** Samuel Richardson publishes *Pamela, or Virtue Rewarded*

1750 · 1760 · 1770 · 1780 · 1790

## Arts and Sciences

1749 Fielding's *Tom Jones* is published

1750 Rousseau wins fame for his *Discourse on the Arts and Sciences*

1751 Voltaire at Frederick the Great's court publishes the *Age of Louis XIV*; Diderot's *Encyclopédie* begins appearing in instalments

1754 Condillac writes *Treatise on the Sensations*

1755 Samuel Johnson publishes his *English Dictionary*

1758 Voltaire moves to Ferney, completes *Candide*

1759 British Museum is opened

1761 Franz Joseph Haydn begins 30-year service with the Esterházys; Rousseau writes his most popular work, *La Nouvelle Hélöise*

1762 Rousseau's masterpieces, *The Social Contract*, and *Emile*, are published; Gluck's *Orfeo ed Euridice* is performed in Vienna

1764 Sterne's *Tristram Shandy*, Winckelmann's *Ancient Art*, Beccaria's *On Crimes and Punishment*, Voltaire's *Philosophical Dictionary*, appear

1767 Lessing publishes *Minna von Barnhelm*; Herder, a leader of *Sturm und Drang*, gains fame with his first writings

1770 Holbach, materialist philosopher, publishes his *System of Nature*

1774 Goethe's *Sorrows of Young Werther* appears

1776 Bentham's *Fragment on Government*, Adam Smith's *Wealth of Nations*, Paine's *Common Sense* and Gibbon's *Decline and Fall of the Roman Empire* (first volume) are published

1778 Voltaire and Rousseau die

1779 Performance of Gluck's *Iphigénie en Tauride* marks the triumph of the new opera form; Hume's *Dialogues Concerning Natural Religion* are published posthumously

1781 Immanuel Kant's *Critique of Pure Reason* appears

1782 Mozart, in Vienna, begins his friendship with Haydn

1784 Beaumarchais' *Marriage of Figaro* performed

1785 Schiller writes *Ode to Joy* and completes *Don Carlos*

1788 Mozart composes his last three symphonies

1789 Lavoisier's *Elementary Treatise on Chemistry*, Bentham's *Principles of Morals and Legislation*, are published

1790 Burke writes *Reflections on the Revolution in France*

1795 Hutton's *Theory of the Earth* is published

1798 Wordsworth and Coleridge publish *Lyrical Ballads*

## History and Politics

1748 Treaty of Aix-la-Chapelle ends War of Austrian Succession, awards Silesia to Frederick the Great

1754 French and Indian War continues English-French rivalry in the New World

1755 Lisbon earthquake lays city in ruins, brings death to 30,000

1756 Diplomatic Revolution leads to the Seven Years' War with Austria and France allied against Prussia and England

1757 Ministry of William Pitt, the Elder, begins; Robert Damiens attempts to assassinate Louis XV

1759 English capture Quebec from the French; Wolfe and Montcalm die in the battle on the Plains of Abraham

1760 King George III begins his 60-year reign

1762 Jesuits are condemned and suppressed in France

1762 Catherine the Great begins her 34-year rule of Russia; Jean Calas is unjustly executed, later declared innocent through Voltaire's efforts

1763 Treaties of Paris and Hubertusburg end Seven Years' War; Prussia becomes a leading power, France loses overseas colonies

1765 Joseph II becomes Emperor and co-regent of Habsburg empire with Empress Maria Theresa; Stamp Act brings resistance in the American colonies

1768 Captain James Cook sails aboard the *Endeavour* on his voyage around the world

1769 Madame du Barry becomes Louis XV's mistress; James Watt patents the improved steam engine

1772 First Partition of Poland by Russia, Prussia and Austria

1773 Jesuit order abolished by the Papacy

1774 Louis XVI and Marie Antoinette become King and Queen of France

1775 Battles of Lexington and Concord begin the American Revolution

1776 Americans issue Declaration of Independence

1778 France joins America as an ally in the War of Independence

1780 First Sunday School is organized by Robert Raikes in England

1781 Joseph II frees the serfs in the Habsburg dominions

1783 Treaty of Paris recognizes an independent United States of America

1785 Diamond Necklace Scandal increases unpopularity of Marie Antoinette

1786 Frederick William II succeeds Frederick the Great in Prussia

1788 Necker becomes France's Director-General of Finance

1789 French Revolution begins; the Bastille is stormed

1792 French Republic is declared by the National Convention

1793 Louis XVI is sentenced and guillotined

1799 Napoleon overthrows the Directory and becomes First Consul

# BIBLIOGRAPHY

*These books were selected during the preparation of the volume for their interest and authority, and for their usefulness to readers seeking additional information on specific points.*

*An asterix (★) marks works available in both hard-cover and paper-back editions; a dagger (†) indicates availability only in paper-back.*

## GENERAL HISTORY

★Clough, Shepard B., and others, *A History of the Western World*. D. C. Heath, 1964.
Durant, Will and Ariel, *The Age of Louis XIV*. Dent, 1963. *The Age of Voltaire*. Dent, 1965.
★Gershoy, Leo, *From Despotism to Revolution; 1763–1789*. Harper & Row, 1944.
★Green, Frederick C., *Eighteenth Century France*. Frederick Ungar, 1965.
★Guérard, Albert, *The Life and Death of an Ideal; France in the Classical Age*. Harper & Row, 1956.
★Knapton, Ernest John, *Europe, 1450–1815*. J. Murray, 1958.
Lacroix, Paul, *France in the Eighteenth Century*. Frederick Ungar, 1963.
★Rowen, Herbert H., *A History of Early Modern Europe, 1500–1815*. Holt, Rinehart & Winston, 1960.
†Rudé, George, *The Eighteenth Century*. Free Press, 1965.
†Smith, Preserved, *Origins of Modern Culture, 1543–1687*. Collier-Macmillan, 1962. *The Enlightenment, 1687–1776*. Collier-Macmillan, 1962.
†Snyder, Louis L., *The Age of Reason*. Van Nostrand, 1955.
Turberville, Arthur Stanley, ed., *Johnson's England: An Account of the Life and Manners of His Age*. 2 vols. Oxford University Press, 1953.

## THOUGHT AND CULTURE

Bruford, W. H., *Germany in the Eighteenth Century: The Social Background of the Literary Revival*. Cambridge University Press, 1952.
★Cazamian, Louis, *History of French Literature*. Oxford University Press, 1955.
†Cragg, Gerald R., *The Church and the Age of Reason*. Hodder, 1962.
Cranston, Maurice William, *John Locke, a Biography*. Longmans, 1957.
★Gay, Peter, *Voltaire's Politics: The Poet as Realist*. Princeton: Oxford University Press, 1959.
Gay, Peter, *The Party of Humanity*. Weidenfeld & Nicolson, 1964.
Green, Frederick, C., *Jean-Jacques Rousseau: A Critical Study of His Life and Writings*. Cambridge University Press, 1955.
★Halévy, Elie, *The Growth of Philosophical Radicalism* (2nd ed.). Transl. by Mary Morris. Faber, 1954.
★Havens, George R., *The Age of Ideas*. P. Owen, 1955.
★Hazard, Paul, *The European Mind: The Critical Years, 1680–1715*. Yale University Press, 1953. *European Thought in the Eighteenth Century from Montesquieu to Lessing*. Meridian Books, 1954.
Legouis, Emile, Louis Cazamian and Raymond Las Vergnas, *History of English Literature* (rev. ed.). Dent, 1965.
★Martin, Kingsley, *French Liberal Thought in the Eighteenth Century; A Study of Political Ideas from Bayle to Condorcet*. Harper & Row, 1962.
Moorman, John R. H., *History of the Church in England*. Black, 1954.
Mossner, Ernest Campbell, *The Life of David Hume*. University of Texas Press, 1954.
Randall, John Herman, Jr., *The Making of the Modern Mind* (rev. ed.). Houghton Mifflin, 1940. *The Career of Philosophy; From the Middle Ages to the Enlightenment*. Columbia University Press, 1962.
Robertson, J. G., *The Life and Work of Goethe, 1749–1832*. E. P. Dutton, 1932. *A History of German Literature* (rev. ed.). Blackwood, 1953.
★Rose, Ernst, *A History of German Literature*. New York University Press: P. Owen, 1960.
Shackleton, Robert, *Montesquieu, A Critical Biography*. Oxford University Press, 1961.
†Stephen, Sir Leslie, *History of English Thought in the Eighteenth Century*. 2 vols. Hart-Davis, 1963.
Trevelyan, George Macaulay, *Illustrated English Social History*. Vol. III, *The*

*Eighteenth Century*. Longmans, 1951.
Turberville, Arthur Stanley, *English Men and Manners in the Eighteenth Century*. Oxford University Press, 1957.
Vartanian, Aram, *La Mettrie's l'Homme Machine: A Study of the Origins of an Idea*. Princeton University Press, 1960.
Wickwar, William Hardy, *Baron d'Holbach; a Prelude to the French Revolution*. London, George Allen & Unwin, Ltd., 1935.
Wilson, Arthur M., *Diderot; The Testing Years, 1713–1759*. Oxford University Press, 1957.

## ECONOMICS

★Ashton, T. S., *The Industrial Revolution, 1760–1830*. Oxford University Press, 1948.
Clough, Shepard B., *The Economic Development of Western Civilization*. McGraw-Hill, 1959.
Gide, Charles and Charles Rist, *A History of Economic Doctrines*. D. C. Heath, 1960.
★Mantoux, Paul, *The Industrial Revolution in the Eighteenth Century* (2nd ed.). Transl. by Marjorie Vernon. Cape, 1961.

## SCIENCE

★Hall, A. R., *The Scientific Revolution, 1500–1800; The Formation of the Modern Scientific Attitude*. Longmans, 1956.
†More, Louis Trenchard, *Isaac Newton, a Biography*. Dover: Constable, 1962.
Murphy, Gardner, *Historical Introduction to Modern Psychology* (rev. ed.). Routledge, 1949.
†Nicolson, Marjorie, *Science and Imagination*. Cornell University Press, 1956.
Wolf, Abraham, *A History of Science, Technology and Philosophy in the 16th and 17th Centuries* (2nd ed.). London, George Allen & Unwin, Ltd., 1961. †*A History of Science, Technology and Philosophy in the 18th Century* (3rd ed.). 2 vols. Allen & Unwin, 1962.

## ART

Adhémar, Jean, *Graphic Art of the 18th Century*. Transl. by M. I. Martin. Thames & Hudson, 1964.
Davenport, Millia, *The Book of Costume*. Crown Publishers, 1965.
Faniel, Stéphane, ed., *French Art of the Eighteenth Century*. Longmans, 1957.
Goncourt, Edmond and Jules de, eds., *French Eighteenth Century Painters*. Phaidon, 1948.
★Savage, George, *Porcelain Through the Ages*. Cassell, 1961.
Schönberger, Arno, and Halldor Soehner, *The Age of the Rococo; Art and Civilization of the 18th Century*. Transl. by Daphne Woodward. McGraw-Hill, 1960.

## MUSIC

★Biancolli, Louis, ed., *The Mozart Handbook*. World Publishing Co., 1954.
Bukofzer, Manfred F., *Music in the Baroque Era*. Dent, 1948.
Carse, Adam, *The Orchestra in the XVIIIth Century*. Cambridge University Press, 1950.
Ferguson, Donald N., *A History of Musical Thought*. Appleton-Century-Crofts, 1948.
Grout, Donald Jay, *A Short History of Opera* (2nd ed.). 2 vols. Columbia University, 1947.
Lang, Paul Henry, *Music in Western Civilization*. Dent, 1942.
Sachs, Curt, *The History of Musical Instruments*. Dent, 1941.

# ART INFORMATION AND PICTURE CREDITS

*The sources for the illustrations in this book are set forth below. Descriptive notes on the works of art are included. Credits for pictures positioned from left to right are separated by semicolons, from top to bottom by dashes. Photographers' names which follow a descriptive note appear in parentheses. Abbreviations include "c." for century and "ca." for circa.*

Cover—*The Geography Lesson* by Pietro Longhi, oil on canvas, *ca.* 1750, Galleria Querini Stampalia, Venice (Scala, Florence). 8-9 Map by David Greenspan.

CHAPTER 1: 10—*Voltaire*, seated figure by Jean-Antoine Houdon, marble, 1781, vestibule of the Théâtre Français, Paris (Gjon Mili). 13—Isaac Newton's original drawing of his reflecting telescope, Royal Society, London (John R. Freeman). 14—Coffeehouse scene, engraving by Henry William Bunbury, 1781, British Museum, London (John R. Freeman). 17—Aerial Voyage by Blanchard and L'Epinard on 26 August, 1785, engraving by unknown artist, late 18th c., courtesy Charles Dolfuss, Paris (Eddy Van der Veen). 19—*Newton* by William Blake, drawing, 1795, courtesy Sir Geoffrey Keynes, London. 21—*Astronomy*, hand-coloured engraving after a mezzotint by Richard Houston, *ca.* 1750, Museum of the History of Science, Oxford (Heinz Zinram). 22-23—Photograph by Roman Vishniac; microscopes, late 17th c. and 18th c., Museum of the History of Science, Oxford (Heinz Zinram)—*Le Jardin des Plantes* by Jean-Baptiste Hilaire, water-colour, 1794, Cabinet des Estampes, Bibliothèque Nationale, Paris. 24—Photograph by William C. Miller, courtesy Mount Wilson and Palomar Observatories—orrery made by Thomas Tompion and George Graham, ebony and silver, *ca.* 1710, Museum of the History of Science, Oxford (Heinz Zinram). 25—*The Orrery* by Joseph Wright of Derby, oil on canvas, *ca.* 1765, Derby Art Gallery, Derby (Derek Bayes). 26—Photograph by Pete Turner from Alpha Photo Associates—*Experiment with an Air Pump* by Joseph Wright of Derby, oil on canvas, 1768, Tate Gallery, London (Derek Bayes). 27—Portrait medal of Antoine Laurent Lavoisier,

Conservatoire des Arts et Métiers, Paris (Pierre Belzeaux from Rapho Guillumette)—water-synthesis apparatus devised by Lavoisier, Conservatoire des Arts et Métiers, Paris (Pierre Belzeaux from Rapho Guillumette). 28-29—Photograph by Richard Jepperson, from Alpha Photo Associates; photograph by Andreas Feininger.

CHAPTER 2: 30—Angel from the Benedictine Abbey of Our Lady, Zwiefalten, Germany, by Johann Michael Feichtmayr and Joseph Christian, 1738-1762 (Dmitri Kessel). 33—*The Pluralist*, engraving by unknown artist, 18th c. (Radio Times Hulton Picture Library, London). 39—Freemason's ceremony, etching by unknown artist, *ca.* 1745, from Hennin Collection Volume 109, Cabinet des Estampes, Bibliothèque Nationale, Paris. 41—*La Promenade à Longchamp* by Gabriel de Saint-Aubin, oil on canvas, 18th c., Musée Hyacinth Rigaud, Perpignan (Pierre Belzeaux from Rapho Guillumette). 42—*Le Lever* designed by Sigmund Freudenberg, engraving, 1774, Print Collection, The Metropolitan Museum of Art, New York (Lee Boltin); *La Toilette* designed by Sigmund Freudenberg, engraving, 1774, Print Collection, The Metropolitan Museum of Art, New York (Lee Boltin)—*La Partie de Whist* designed by Jean-Michel Moreau le jeune, engraving, 1776, Print Collection, The Metropolitan Museum of Art, New York (Robert Kafka). 43—*La Promenade du Matin* designed by Sigmund Freudenberg, engraving, 1774, Print Collection, The Metropolitan Museum of Art, New York (Lee Boltin); *L'Accord Parfait* designed by Jean-Michel Moreau le jeune, engraving, 1776, Print Collection, The Metropolitan Museum of Art, New York (Lee Boltin)—*Les Confidences* designed by Sigmund Freudenberg, engraving, 1774, Print Collection, The Metropolitan Museum of Art, New York (Lee Boltin); *Oui Ou Non* designed by Jean-Michel Moreau le jeune, engraving 1776, Print Collection, The Metropolitan Museum of Art, New York (Lee Boltin). 44–45—*Madame de Pompadour* by François Boucher or atelier, oil on canvas, mid-18th c., Louvre Museum, Paris (Eric Schaal); *Bal Masqué à la Galerie des Glaces* by Charles Nicolas Cochin, *fils*, gouache sketch, mid-18th c., Louvre Museum, Paris (Giraudon)—*Le Souper Fin* designed by Jean-Michel Moreau le jeune, coloured engraving, 1776. 46–47—*The Salon of Madame Geoffrin* by Anicet Lemonnier, oil on canvas, 1814, Musée des Beaux Arts, Rouen (Giraudon). 48–49—*La Petite Loge* designed by Jean-Michel Moreau le jeune, engraving, 1776, Print Collection, The Metropolitan Museum of Art, New York (Lee Boltin)—*Mlle Sophie Arnould* by Jean-Baptiste Greuze, oil on canvas, *ca.* 1773, reproduced by permission of the Trustees of the Wallace Collection, London (Derek Bayes); *Fête à Saint-Cloud* by Jean-Honoré Fragonard, oil on canvas, *ca.* 1775, courtesy of the Banque de France, Paris. 50—*Le Bouquet* designed by Charles Eisen, coloured engraving, 1756. 51—*Les Délices de la Maternité* designed by Jean-Michel Moreau le jeune, engraving, 1776, Print Collection, The Metropolitan Museum of Art, New York (Lee Boltin).

CHAPTER 3: 52—*Fête de l'Etre suprême Célébre au Champ de Mars, le 8 Juin, 1794* by Thomas Charles Naudet, gouache and aquarelle, Musée Carnavalet (Horizon). 57—Caricature of John Wilkes by William Hogarth, etching, 1763, Print Room, New York Public Library (Werner Wolff from Black Star). 58—Portrait of Voltaire at the age of 24, engraving by J. Mollison after original oil painting by Nicolas de Largillière (Culver Pictures). 60—Porcelain vase from the Lund factory, Bristol, *ca.* 1750, courtesy of the Syndics of the Fitzwilliam Museum, Cambridge (Derek Bayes). 63—Engraving by Jean-Michel Moreau le jeune for *Les Incas* by Jean-François Marmontel, 1777, Print Collection, The Metropolitan Museum of Art, New York (Frank Lerner). 65—*Metallic Tractors* designed by James Gilray, satiric print, 1801, British Museum, London (John R. Freeman). 66–67—*The Hypnotist* by Daniel Chodowiecki, etching, *ca.* 1790 (The Bettmann Archive); *Animal Magnetism*, engraving, 18th c. (Culver Pictures)—*The Quintessence of Quackism*, English satirical print, 1780 (Radio Times Hulton Picture Library, London). 68–69—Johann Kaspar Lavater at work in his study, engraving from his *Physiognomische Fragmente zur Beförderung der Menschenkenntnis und Menschenliebe*, 1776, Radio Times Hulton Picture Library (Derek Bayes); four illustrations from Johann Kaspar Lavater's *Physiognomische Fragmente zur Beförderung der Menschenkenntnis und Menschenliebe*, 1776, Bayerische Staatsbibliothek, Munich; silhouette of Johann Wolfgang von Goethe (Historisches Bildarchiv, Bad Berneck). 70–71—*Mary Tofts Giving Birth to Rabbits* by William Hogarth, engraving, 1727, British Museum (John R. Freeman)—*Cagliostro at the Lodge of Antiquity*, 18th-c. French engraving (Radio Times Hulton Picture Library, London); presumed portrait of Casanova, 18th-c. cartoon (The Bettmann Archive). 72–73—Three Shakespeare forgeries by William Ireland, 1795 (Radio Times Hulton Picture Library, London); fossil illustrations from Johann Beringer's *Lithographia Wirceburgensis*, first published 1728, British Museum, London. 74–75—John Law in a Cart, engraving from Dutch satirical work, *Het Groote Tafereel der Dwaasheid* (The Great Mirror of Folly), 1720, New York Public Library—Bombario, detail of engraving from *Het Groote Tafereel der Dwaasheid* (The Great Mirror of Folly), 1720, Guildhall Library, London (Alan Clifton); *The South Sea Bubble* by William Hogarth, engraving, 1721.

CHAPTER 4: 76—Folk-gathering by Daniel Chodowiecki, etching, late 18th c., Print Collection, The Metropolitan Museum of Art, New York (Frank Lerner). 78—Cover of *The Gentleman's Magazine*, January 1731, British Museum, London. 82—*Hall's Library at Margate*, aquatint by T. Malton, 1789, British Museum (John R. Freeman). 84–85—Plates from *Encyclopédie, ou Dictionnaire raisonné des sciences, des arts et des métiers*, edited by Denis Diderot and Jean Le Rond d'Alembert, first edition, 1751, New York Public Library. 87—*Thomas William Coke, Earl of Leicester* by Pompeo Girolamo Batoni, oil on canvas, 1774, courtesy the Earl of Leicester, Holkham Hall, Norfolk (Derek Bayes). 88–89—Map by Etienne Delessert. 90–91—*Celebration in the Paris Markets at the Birth of the Dauphin* by Philibert-Louis Debucourt, oil on canvas, 1782, Musée Carnavalet, Paris (Eric Schaal)—*View of the Palace of Versailles* by Pierre-Denis Martin, oil on canvas, 1722, Versailles National Museum (Eddy Van der Veen). 92–93—Diagram by Matt Greene; *Tribuna of the Uffizi* by Johann Zoffany, oil on canvas, *ca.* 1775, Royal Collection, Windsor (Photo A. C. Cooper, colour, Ltd. Copyright Reserved). 94–95—*Regatta on the Grand Canal* by Canaletto (Antonio Canale), oil on canvas, *ca.* 1730, Royal Collection, Windsor (Photo A. C. Cooper, colour, Ltd. Copyright-Reserved.)—*The Charlatan* by Giandomenico Tiepolo, oil on canvas, 1754, Louvre Museum, Paris (Eric Schaal); Interior of St. Mark's Cathedral, Venice by Canaletto (Antonio Canale), oil on canvas, *ca.* 1755, Royal Collection, Windsor. 96—Scene at Mount Vesuvius by Pietro Fabris, tempera, *ca.* 1775, collection of Baron Lemmerman, Rome (Emmett Bright); scene of excavation at Pompeii by Pietro Fabris tempera, *ca.* 1775, collection of Baron Lemmerman, Rome (Emmett Bright). 97—*Interior of the Antiquary's Shop, Naples* by an unknown Neapolitan, 1798, collection of Manlio Goffi, Rome (Ettore Naldoni). 98–99—*Interior of St. Peter's by* Giovanni Paolo Pannini, oil on canvas, 1755, Niedersächsisches Landesmuseum, Hanover (Robert Lackenbach from Black Star).

CHAPTER 5: 100—Engine erected by Martin Triewald at Dannemora, Sweden, in 1727, engraving, 1734, The Science Museum, London. 103—Detail of plate from *Encyclopédie ou Dictionnaire raisonné des sciences, des arts et des métiers*, edited by Denis Diderot and Jean Le Rond d'Alembert, first edition, 1751, New York Public Library. 105—Diagram by Otto Van Eersel. 106—Diagram by Otto Van Eersel. 108—*Panopticon*, model prison designed by Jeremy Bentham, British Museum, London (John R. Freeman). 111 to 119—*The Rake's Progress* by William Hogarth, oil on canvas, 1730's, courtesy Trustees of Sir John Soane's Museum, London (Derek Bayes).

CHAPTER 6: 120—Photograph by Erich Lessing from Magnum. 123—Illustrations for *Le Maitre à Danser* by Pierre Rameau, 1734, New York Public Library. 125—*A Side-Box at the Opera*, from *A Collection of Political Caricatures, Broadsides, Portraits, 1642–1830, from the library of Sir Robert Peel, Bart.*, Volume V, the Pierpont Morgan Library (Werner Wolff from Black Star). 126—First page of *Minuet and Trio for Pianoforte* by Wolfgang Amadeus Mozart, 1762, City Museum, Salzburg (Gjon Mili). 129—Court Theatre at Schönbrunn, Vienna (Erich Lessing from Magnum). 130–131—The Tschudi Family, artist unknown, *ca.* 1745, collection of Captain Evelyn Broadwood, M. C., Surrey (Derek Bayes)—diagrams by John and Mary Condon; pianoforte made by Johann Jacob Könicke, Vienna, 1795, Yale University, School of Music, Collection of Musical Instruments (Ken Kay). 132–133—Wolfgang Amadeus Mozart with father Leopold and sister Nannerl by Louis Carrogis de Carmontelle, water-colour, 1764, courtesy Philip Hill (Derek Bayes); *The Cowper and Gore Families* by Johann Zoffany, oil on canvas, 1772–1773, courtesy Lady Salmond (The Medici Society, London). 134–135—Oboe made by Johann Ferdinand Floth, Dresden, *ca.* 1800, Yale University, School of Music, Collection of Musical Instruments (Ken Kay); viola made by unknown English artist, *ca.* 1800, Yale University, School of Music, Collection of Musical Instruments (Ken Kay); illustration by Nicholas Fasciano—Franz Joseph Haydn conducting an opera at Esterhaz, gouache, *ca.* 1755, Theater Museum, Munich (Walter Sanders). 136–137—Costume design by Antoine Daniel Bertoli, first half of 18th c., Archiv für Kunst und Geschichte, Berlin; stage design by Alessandro Galli da Bibiena, gouache, mid-18th c., Staatliche Graphische Sammlung, Munich (Friedrich Rauch)—Residenztheater, Munich, copper etching, 1721, Theater Museum, Munich (Friedrich Rauch). 138–139—Christoph Willibald Gluck at the spinet by Josèphe-Sifrède Duplessis, oil on canvas, 1775, Kunsthistorisches Museum, Vienna; photograph by Jochen Blume.

CHAPTER 7: 140—*Voltaire and Frederick the Great*, engraving by Pierre-Louis Baquoy after a drawing by Nicolas Monsiaux, *ca.* 1795, Bibliothèque Nationale, Paris (Bulloz). 143—Plate from plans and sections for the Imperial Academy of Sciences at St. Petersburg, 1741, Burndy Library, Norwalk (Albert Fenn). 145—Dutchman (komojin zu) by Matsui Genchu, colour on paper, mid-18th c., Kobe Municipal Museum, Japan (Bradley Smith). 148–149—*Versuch, auf den Parnass zu gelangen*, illustration from *Ansichten der Literatur und Kunst unseres Zeitalters*, I. Heft, 1803, courtesy Goethe House, New York. 151—*The Philosophers at Supper* by Jean Huber, engraving, mid-18th c., Bibliothèque Nationale (Eddy Van der Veen). 152 to 163—Plates from *Encyclopédie, ou Dictionnaire raisonné des sciences, des arts et des métiers*, edited by Denis Diderot and Jean Le Rond d'Alembert, first edition, 1751, New York Public Library.

CHAPTER 8: 164—*The Pottery Merchants* by Francisco José de Goya, cartoon for a tapestry, 1779, Prado Museum, Madrid (Augusto Meneses). 169—*Salottino di Porcellana*, porcelain salon made 1757–1759, Capodimonte Museum, Naples (Emmett Bright). 170–171—Detail from an armoire, oak, French Regency period, 1715–1723, The Metropolitan Museum of Art, New York, Rogers Fund, 1919 (Henry Groskinsky); detail of leg of carved and gilded armchair, by Georges Jacob, French, 1780, The Metropolitan Museum of Art, New York, gift of the Samuel H. Kress Foundation, 1958 (Henry Groskinsky); detail from roll-top desk, marquetried chinoiserie scene of satinwood and green stained wood on a ground of harewood, by David Roentgen, Germany 1775–1780, The Metropolitan Museum of Art, New York, Rogers Fund, 1941 (Henry Groskinsky). 172–173—Snuff box, made for the Duke of Choiseul, decorated with gouaches by Louis-Nicolas van Blarenberghe, *ca.* 1770, private collection, Paris (Sabine Weiss from Rapho Guillumette). 174–175—Detail from *Girl Frightened by a Snake* after *La Surprise* by Clodion, hard-paste porcelain, German, *ca.* 1770, The Metropolitan Museum of Art, New York, gift of R. Thornton Wilson in memory of Florence Ellsworth Wilson, 1950 (Arnold Newman); *The Merchant*, hard-paste porcelain, German, *ca.* 1765, The Metropolitan Museum of Art, New York, gift of R. Thornton Wilson in memory of Florence Ellsworth Wilson, 1943 (Arnold Newman). 176–177—Tapestry room from Croome Court, Worcestershire, made by Gobelins, 1764–1771, The Metropolitan Museum of Art, New York, gift of the Samuel H. Kress Foundation, 1958 (Arnold Newman). 178—*Nécessaire*, gold and agate, English, mid-18th c., The Metropolitan Museum of Art, New York, gift of Admiral F. R. Harris in memory of his wife, Dena Sperry Harris, 1946 (Richard Meek). 179—Egg-cup, silver, French, *ca.* 1725, The Metropolitan Museum of Art, New York, Bequest of Catherine D. Wentworth, 1948 (Richard Meek); detail from a glove tray, silver, French, *ca.* 1723, The Metropolitan Museum of Art, New York, Bequest of Catherine D. Wentworth, 1948 (Richard Meek). 180–181—*Trionfo da Tavola* (Table Triumph), made for the Palazzo Morosini, Venice, glass, 8 by 5 feet, 18th c., Museo Vetrario, Murano (Erich Lessing from Magnum).

# ACKNOWLEDGEMENTS

The editors of this book are particularly indebted to Herbert H. Rowen, Professor of History, Rutgers, The State University, New Brunswick, N.J.; Joseph W. Reed, Assistant Professor of English, Wesleyan University, Middletown, Conn.; Frederick Kilgour, Associate Librarian, Yale University Library, New Haven, Conn.; The Rev. Wilhelm Pauck, Professor of Church History, Union Theological Seminary, New York; Ellen Wagner, Publicity Department, The Metropolitan Museum of Art; Bern Dibner and Adele Matthysee, The Burndy Library, Norwalk, Conn.; Joel Sachs; Matila Simon; Cabinet des Dessins du Musée du Louvre; Madame Le Monnier, Service Photographique de la Bibliothèque Nationale; The Department of Prints and Drawings, British Museum, London; The Derby Museum and Art Gallery, The Earl of Leicester, Holkham Hall, Norfolk; The Librarian, The Guildhall Library, London; Worcester College Library, Oxford; The Royal Copenhagen Porcelain Company, Ltd., London; Theater Museum, Munich; Bayerische Staatsbibliothek, Munich; Archiv für Kunst und Geschichte, Berlin; Historisches Bildarchiv, Bad Berneck; Deutsches Opernhaus, Berlin; Felice Battaglia, Rector, Università Bologna; Lamberto Coppini, Istituto di Anatomia, Bologna; Maria Luisa Bonelli, Director, Museo di Storia della Scienza, Florence; Lamberto Scotti, Teatro Comunale, Florence; Clelia Alberici, Director, Civica Raccolta Bertarelli, Milan; Luigi Belloni, Università degli Studi, Milan; Maria-Grazia Santarelli, Longanesi & C., Milan; Raffaello Causa, Soprintendente alle Gallerie per la Campania, Naples; Bruno Malajoli, Director of Fine Arts for Italy, Ministero di Pubblica Istruzione, Rome; Manlio Goffi, Rome; Baron Basile Lemmerman, Rome; Carla Mancini, Biblioteca Nazionale, Rome; Mario Praz, Università degli Studi, Rome; Noemi Gabrielli, Soprintendente alle Gallerie del Piemonte, Turin; Giovanni Mariacher, Superintendent, Terisio Pignatti, Lucia Casanova and Narciso Stefani, Museo Correr, Venice; and Aldo Soppelsa, Museo Vetrario, Murano, Venice.

# INDEX

**XXXXXXXXX**
*Typesetting by Hazell Watson & Viney Ltd., Aylesbury*
*Printed in Spain by Novograph, S. A., Madrid*
*Bound by Roner, S. A., Madrid*
*Depósito Legal: M-2353-XXVI*